C000130189

INTRODUCING MALLY WELBURN

This is Mally Welburn's first book. It will not be his last.

Mally isn't an accomplished writer yet, he'd be the first to admit that.

He's a rough diamond - a unique storyteller, with a unique story.

Reading 'Mally - The Boy Who Flew Through Windows' is rather like living Mally's life, or at least selected episodes of it, all over again.

He retraces snapshots of his very eventful life through graphically truthful extracts, tied together by a blunt, down to earth style.

In 'Part One' of his story Mally opens with a modern day introduction.

In the opening chapters, he describes his love for 'his new life', his recently discovered ability to laugh and a freshly found confidence that he'd previously lacked.

These are soon eclipsed however by darker tales as he takes us back to the sixties and seventies to re-live his childhood in the backstreets of Hull.

The contrast between the two eras is a vivid one.

One page is heartbreakingly tragic and disturbing, the next side-splittingly funny.

At times you won't know whether to laugh or cry - or both.

One thing is certain however - you won't have read a book like this before…

MALLY

PART ONE:

THE BOY WHO FLEW
THROUGH WINDOWS

**RIVERHEAD
PUBLISHING**

MALLY WELBURN

First published in Great Britain in 2006
by Riverhead Publishing

A CIP catalogue record for this book is
available from the British Library.

ISBN 0-9550237-1-8

Typeset in Times New Roman by
Riverhead Publishing, Hull, East Yorkshire.

Printed by
Fretwells Limited, Oslo Road, Hull, HU7 0YN.

Designed by Riverhead Publishing

Thankyou for purchasing this book.
By doing so you have already helped the NSPCC as a
donation will be made to that charity for every copy of
'MALLY - The Boy Who Flew Through Windows' sold.

You can find out more about future books by
Mally Welburn on: www.riverheadonline.co.uk

CONTENTS

1 HERE COMES THE SUN................ 7
2 KNOCK KNOCK WHO'S THERE? 22
3 TAKE A CHANCE ON ME.............. 37
4 ONLY THE LONELY...................... 57
5 ROAD TO NOWHERE.................... 69
6 TEENAGE RAMPAGE.................... 85
7 RIDE A WHITE SWAN................... 97
8 STAYIN' ALIVE............................. 113
9 PUT YOURSELF IN MY PLACE.... 127
10 YOU'RE THE FIRST,
   THE LAST, MY EVERYTHING..... 145
11 BREAKING UP IS HARD TO DO... 159

DEDICATION

This book is dedicated to my dear late Mother, Ada,
without whose love and care I undoubtedly wouldn't still be
here to tell this story.
To my two daughters, Tammie and Keelie
my son, Peter and my two grandsons, Kailem and Aydan.

WE'RE SO PROUD OF YOU DAD

Wow! what a book! I can honestly say I'd have never thought
my Dad had been through so much pain,
being the man he is today.
He is such an inspiration to me and I'm so proud of who he
has become. It just goes to show you can turn your life around
whatever the circumstances.
Well done Dad. Love you loads - Keelie Marie.

You have survived these unimaginable and degrading actions,
forced upon you as a boy by the hands of many evil men.
You are a true life inspiration and I'm so proud and honoured
to call you my Dad.
Your ever-loving daughter - Tammie Marie.

What a totally gripping and outstanding story of triumph over
true adversity.
Well done 'Mally me Dad' - loving son, Peter.

CHAPTER ONE
HERE COMES THE SUN

I woke up in the middle of the night. It was pitch black! Something was moving on the blanket at the bottom of my bed. Within a second or two I was wide awake!

The adrenaline was already pumping! My eyes, quickly growing used to the darkness. I raised my head off the pillow, hoping the mysterious, black shape I could just make out at the foot of my bed wouldn't notice my movement. I tried to focus on whatever it was. It appeared to be about a foot high and about two feet long. It was nuzzling between my feet. First it nudged my right ankle and then it brushed heavily against my left leg. Whatever had joined me in my 'cave' was obviously of considerable size and weight. I don't mind admitting I was scared shitless!

My heart was pounding and even though it was November and the room was well below freezing, sweat was already running down my face. My breath hovered over my head in the chilly, night air, like a dark mist. I tried to stay calm and convince myself that my 'unwanted visitor' was only a stray cat that had found its way in out of the cold winter night. But deep down of course I already knew exactly what it was - the biggest, blackest, fucking rat I'd ever seen in my life!

Well, what do you do in a situation like that? There were three options. As they'd put it in a TV quiz, I could:

(a) - grit my teeth, get up - and rip its head off!

(b) - remain perfectly still and hope it went away - or

(c) - dive out of the bed and run as fucking fast as I could!

It only took me a fraction of a second to decide on option c! In one movement, that wouldn't have looked out of place in the latest Superman film, I leapt out from under my covers, raced barefoot across the floor, dived straight through the window and landed in the yard outside!

There was glass everywhere! But that didn't bother me. I was

7

used to flying through windows. I'd been doing it since I was five years old...

I quickly picked up the biggest brick I could lay my hands on and crept back to the broken window. Peering into the gloomy interior, I could make out the shape of my bed and my table and my chair. But there was no sign of the fucking rat!

I didn't know whether that was a good thing or not. Had it ran out as quickly as I had? Or was it still in the room somewhere, lurking in the shadows?

I realised I didn't need to know the answer to that particular question, at least not at that exact moment!

I'd had enough action for one night. I decided to stay outside in the yard until it got light.

I'd never classed myself as a coward, far from it in fact, as you'll learn later. But there was no way I was going back into that building to face what must have been the biggest rat in the world, when I didn't have to!

I sat and watched the frost glistening in the moonlight for between two or three hours. At the time it seemed a lot longer. But I was quite happy - and safe - sheltering under a piece of tarpaulin. I didn't feel the cold at all - I never have...

That wasn't the only rat I've encountered during my forty-eight years. Unfortunately there have been many, many more. Do you know that no matter wherever you are in an English city, you're never more than thirty feet away from one. That may seem quite a sobering thought and hard to believe for most people but it never surprised me. I've been surrounded by rats of varying types and descriptions all my life. And I'd lived for years with the biggest rat of them all - my own Dad...

That incident with the rat is the first of many you'll read about in the following chapters. It happened over two years ago now but it seems like only yesterday. I was living in my 'cave' at the time.

You may have already noticed a few swear words in the opening paragraphs. I'll tell you now there are a lot more in the rest of the book. I make no apology for that. I realise swearing isn't clever and is more often than not usually down to the fact that the person simply can't be bothered to think of other words to use. But this is my story about my life. And the people in my life used that language all the time.

I'm not trying to sound offensive but simply reflecting the incidents and the characters as accurately and authentically as I can.

I've included some disturbing accounts of what happened to me as a boy and a teenager. Again I've simply told them as they happened and how I still remember them to this day. When you read them I'm sure you'll agree the language used is an integral part of their impact, their violence, their humour and of the characters involved.

I wrote this book to help to release all the demons that have burdened me throughout my life. I realise the problems I've faced and the abuse I suffered undoubtedly moulded me into the character I became. But I wanted to prove that no matter how tragic an upbringing you have, there's always a way out. There's always a solution to your problems, if you're determined enough to find it. I wanted to show that it's possible for everyone to make something of their life, no matter how bad the hand of cards they were originally dealt may have been.

Your destiny is not pre-ordained. You can change it!

I won't deny, for years I struggled to find the right path. For years I made the wrong decisions. I'll tell you about them all. But at the age of forty - yes the big 40 - I made a conscious decision that the second part of my life, no matter how long that turns out to be, would be significantly better than the first. I'd been to approved schools. I'd stayed in detention centres. I'd been locked up in prison with some of the worst people imaginable! It was time for that change!

A leopard can't change its spots, said some. But it's never too late to change, said others. I'd like you to decide who was right. And if my story can somehow help just one person who may have gone off the rails somewhere along his life's journey, to put their problems into perspective, then it will have been worthwhile putting pen to paper. Or in my case, finger to keyboard. I'll let you decide...

I hope my story will also make you think about how well off you are. And how lucky you've been to be born and brought up by people who loved and cared for you. The chances are you've had a good upbringing and a happy childhood. I hope so. But before you start to argue that there are thousands of people who have probably had far worse to put up with than I did, I'll say I wouldn't deny that for a second. I'm not saying my childhood was the worst upbringing anyone could ever have had. What I intend to point out is that you can have the worst start in life, suffer all the neglect and abuse imaginable - and still survive it and make something of your life.

I've wasted a lot of my life. Only in the last few years have I started to realise that I could get something worthwhile out of it. And that I could make something of myself. That finally, I wanted to get up in the morning. There were things I had to do. Goals I wanted to achieve.

I didn't want to end my days being known as that lad who was unloved and abused and ended up in childrens' homes and then approved schools. I didn't want people to remember me as that delinquent teenager who went off the rails. Or as the no-hoper who ended up fighting nearly every day of his life. Or as the lad who got his girlfriend pregnant just before she 'dumped' him. Or as the thug who ended up in borstal. And then prison. Or the man who nearly drank himself into an early grave. Or the loser who got divorced and ended up with what he'd started out with twenty-odd years earlier - nothing! Only in the last few years have I started to live. And only in the last few years have I learned to laugh!

Whoever said, 'Life begins at forty,' certainly knew what they were talking about. I only hope they hadn't to suffer a life like mine to be able to make that assertion.

You can turn your life around no matter how bad it is or how old you are. It's never too late. Life can begin at forty - or any other age - I made sure it did for me...

Don't get me wrong, the first few years of 'my new life' weren't easy. At times, things ran far from smoothly. Some happenings in 'my new life' were totally unplanned. And I soon found that running a business and taking risks, can sometimes bring disappointments.

I had my share of ups and downs. I had to live in my 'cave'. I had disagreements with business colleagues. And I even lost the firm that I'd created for a while. Finally, I had a 'dream' that didn't work out as I hoped it would. And I went back to square one and started again!

All those problems were part of life's learning curve. It was a new curve to me. One that I've been making my way along only since I was forty. Twenty years or so later than most other people!

I'd wasted those twenty years. In detention centres! In prison! In a failing marriage! Risking my life at sea! Boozing! Fighting! Getting divorced! More Boozing! More Fighting! Going nowhere! Useless!

Things are very different now! And most importantly - I'm happier now than I've ever been! I've been flying through windows all my life. Now, I'm glad to say the windows are ones of opportunity. Times have changed. But before we go any further I'd better tell you a little bit about myself.

My name's Mally Welburn. I'm forty-eight years of age. But at this moment in my life I feel like a thirty-year-old! But there's none about - females that is.

Saying that, I'm not ready to be chained down again yet! Don't knock it until you try it, that's what I say.

I need to tell you about myself - a bit at a time, that is. I think you'll like to read about the 'bounce-back kid'. The one that has that bounce-back ability! Yes, that would be me. Let me tell you where I am at this moment in time in my life.

The date is November 5, Bonfire Night, 2004. And I'm sat in my office come home.

The cave I call it, I feel like - was it Robert The Bruce? You know, the guy who was losing the battle and so he retreated to an old cottage - his 'cave' - to plan what to do next. He thought he had lost the battle, you know he had lost his men, his army, then he went into his 'cave' - darkness - well life can be like that, can't it? We all get knock-backs in life. It's how you bounce back that counts. And how you learn from your knock-backs. As the saying goes, a day without learning is a day wasted.

Well let me tell you about some of the wasted days I've had in my life, and how it's got me to be this one fingered man on this out of date computer - but I love learning how to use it.

Well anyway, where was I?

A big firework has just gone off outside. Life can be like a firework, and so can people, can't they?

What firework would you be? I think I would be that rocket! You know, reach for the moon and you'll fall among those

MALLY - THE BOY WHO FLEW THROUGH WINDOWS

stars. Well, that's what I've been trying to do for the last six or seven years...

Let me tell you a true story.

As I said, I'm forty-eight years old. Well, eight of those years ago I decided to do something with my life. Because at the time, I thought that I was a social outcast.

Why? I hear you ask.

Well, up to the age of forty, my life consisted of an endless trek down every wrong road imaginable. Most of my childhood, I spent unhappy and afraid. What a nightmare!

I was one of eight brothers and I'm also a twin. When I was born I'm sure I got dragged out with my feet first. I now take a size 14 in shoes.

You know what they say about men with big feet, don't you? Well in my case it's a lie. Saying that I had to share what I got with my twin brother. I got the feet. I won't tell you what he got but he's got a couple more inches of it than I have in the lunchbox department, the bastard! But if it hadn't been for him, I suppose I wouldn't be so good looking and blessed with the gift of the gab!

When you're one of eight lads - it's a life of hand-me-downs - 'first up - best dressed'. When you had to wear those trousers that yer brother had worn without them being washed for most probably a month or more. But wearing someone else's trousers didn't hurt me. It was my father that hurt me.

And the hurt he did to my mother, bless her! My mother was the most loving woman you could have wished to meet. And the beatings she took for us were unreal. You wouldn't believe me if I told you, but you'll get the picture as we go along.

Later on those wrong roads led me to remand homes and detention centres. And finally to alcohol abuse and prison!

Who do you blame?

Do you blame your upbringing? I don't know!

Some people try to bury the past but I believe it makes you what you are today. Sometimes the past helps, sometimes it doesn't! In my case it's been a bit of both.

I'll tell you a little later about how all those events affected me. But to start with I'd like to tell you about what I've been doing in the last few years.

I'd like to start by telling you what life was like in my 'cave' with Robert The Bruce - and his spider.

We all know the story of Robert The Bruce, don't we? He was sat in his 'cave' and he looked up and saw the spider trying to get across the roof by using his web. Again and again the spider tried. And again and again the wind kept blowing the spider back. Six times he tried and six times he was blown back. But on the seventh attempt the spider succeeded.

Robert The Bruce got inspiration from that spider in his 'cave' and so did I.

Everybody has their 'cave' don't they?

Your cave can simply be a room, a shed or a hideaway. It can be a comfortable retreat or a snug little den. In my case, it was none of these! I didn't have a 'home'. At least I didn't have a traditional home where I could go at the end of the day when I finished work. That loving home. All I had when I moved in was a nearly derelict, concrete building!

I'd previously been in two or three other 'caves' but the Hull City Council gave me this particular one. It consisted of half an acre of land with a factory, a building, sort of like a garage and this office.

I'd been looking for suitable premises to expand my business, which was building fences and sheds out of reclaimed timber and discarded pallets. Not the little pallets, the big ones that they delivered poly-carbonate sheets on. Some were thirty foot long by eight foot wide. And you'd get thirty boards on those and eight, eight-foot, four by four posts - there's your fencing.

But then the foot and mouth came along and they started to take all my pallets off me to use for the burning of the sheep. Which drove me to the position where I was in my little 'cave' with nothing much to do.

When the council first gave me the keys to it, I was like a kid in a sweet shop to be honest. I had all my plans. I never had many belongings. And at first we stayed in the garage, all I had was an old bed mattress and a couch, or should we call it a settee? But I got a caravan after our first couple of nights in there cos what the council didn't tell me was that the place was overrun with rats. So me and my friend moved in there after a couple of days moving in our wood and machinery.

We started to 'camp' there - me and one of the lads who

worked with me, Joe Beaumont. I said to him we'll crash out here. I must stress there were no lights - it was November and pitch black!

It got dark by five o'clock. We were camping down in the disused garage. And as you'll find out I love my chocolate. Mars bars - and I'm into Cadbury's Whole Nut as well. I'd eaten half a bar of this Whole Nut and whilst I was asleep I had the half-eaten bar beside me. It was about six or seven o'clock in the morning, just starting to get light. There were no doors on the place so whatever bit of daylight there was, was coming in. And I heard the crackling of paper.

I opened my eyes to see the biggest rat I'd ever seen, nibbling at my chocolate bar. I was laid on the floor, and only four inches away, the thickness of a mattress, was this rat staring me right in the face!

Well I was brought up with rats, but this was that big that at first I thought it was a 'fat cat' to be honest.

With that I put my arm across onto Joe on the couch, who I found out was already awake. He said: 'I've seen it!' And he leapt over me to try and catch it. It ran out into the yard and he chased it all over before it disappeared down this hole.

He was trying to get his arm down the hole to catch the rat. Fortunately he didn't succeed!

When he came back, I noticed he was itching his arm. We rolled his sleeve up and he shouted,

'Fucking hell! Look at that!'

There was this bug that had buried itself in his arm. It was over an inch long. I'd never seen anything like it in my life. It was some sort of beetle. It was buried in his skin. We got a pair of pliers and pulled the back end of it out. And he had to go to hospital to get it attended to properly. He had it cut out and had a load of injections for virtually every disease you could think of.

After less than a week in that yard, Joe left.

He didn't want anything else to do with it.

I never saw him again.

So I was left on my own. I decided to get a little caravan. And I got two abandoned dogs as well, Cassie and Max.

Max was an old lad about fourteen and we thought Cassie was only about two. She'd play with the rats and catch them. And when a customer came into the yard she'd drop a rat at their feet. Buy one, get one free, I used to say, the rat's free...

I got my vision of the football shed - 'The Dream' - whilst I was living in the caravan and trying to save my reclaimed timber business.

The only reason I'd moved in was because I'd got the yard for a peppercorn rent as the place was in such a bad state.

There was no electric, no running water, rats everywhere, when it rained the factory flooded - all the drains were blocked and when you had a shit it would float back up! It was a real 'shitehole' - but from then on the Council kept saying that I could have it for another six months rent free.

After a particularly bad bit of weather, when there was a lot of damage caused to the property and all the asbestos sheets were blown off the roof, I complained again. They turned round and said,

'Do you want to buy it off us for twenty-five grand?'

I didn't have twenty-five quid!

I'd only been in business for a year or two and things were going far from well. So I went to see a friend, Charles Crannon, at Dutch Imports and he said he'd give me the twenty-five grand to buy it with.

'You can stay in it for another year rent-free,' he said.

'But after that time it will be £250 a week.'

It was a good investment for him. That yard today, that he still owns, is worth about £250,000!

So sometimes you miss the little trick, don't ya?

He also owns some little units off St James Street and the deal was when I gave up the yard he'd put me in one of the units for £50 a week. I'm now tendering for a piece of land at the back of the yard. And when I get that it will be mine to sell on. That's my payback! But that's another story...

Joe and his fright with the burrowing bug wasn't the only problem that we encountered when we first moved into the yard. There was a far more terrifying one for me!

Whilst I was making the building habitable, I moved my little caravan into the yard with me as a makeshift mobile home.

It was whilst I was camping in the van that I came up with my idea for 'The Dream' - but more about that later.

The previous occupants of the yard before me, used the

premises to produce carved marble headstones and some locals said the place was haunted. Rumour had it that two people had hung themselves in the factory and their spirits apparently still haunted the yard. Even the council said that they'd had numerous reports of inexplicable 'goings-on'. To make things even 'spookier' there was no electricity in the place. And no lights in the street outside, St James Street, off English Street, dead-end street, west Hull!

A high, wooden fence with lots of holes in it surrounded the whole place. And propped all around the perimeter fence were all these headstones, some dating back to the turn of the last century. 'In loving memory of Christine so and so - died March 14, 1912' - really old stones. One night, it was pitch black, I was in my caravan when I heard:

Ooooohhh! Ooooohhh!

I thought, what the fuck's that? I was in the caravan on my tod. At least until Cassie ran in and hid under the little table in the corner. But the old dog was left outside, he couldn't get up the steps. He just went, woof! woof! He only had a really quiet old bark on him. So I crept outside of the caravan which was parked up against the fence - and I heard it again.

Ooooohhh! Ooooohhh!

I thought, shit! I was a bit frightened as it was going through my head about the two people who'd hung themselves there - and that the place was reported to be haunted. I walked out in my bare feet. It was drizzling and a bit misty that night.

The noise was coming from a headstone. As I looked closer there was also steam coming off it!

I went a little bit nearer and heard it again.

Ooooohhh! I thought what the fuck is that?

But as I got virtually up to it I heard.

'Ooooohhh! go on love and I'll give you another twenty quid!'

The mystery was solved!

The street was where all the prostitutes used to bring their punters! And the 'ghostly' sounds were simply the noises of them doing 'it' against me fence! But once I knew what was going on, it turned into a little money spinner for me as well. I've sold that many sheds since through a little hole in me fence. It used to be a little hobby of mine - just looking through this little hole and waiting for those punters to come on the 'quick strokes'. Then I'd bang on the fence and say, That's a waste of fifty quid mate - and slot my card through! I've sold loads of sheds through that little hole in me fence...

I'd often make additional trips to see the Council and even take the dead rats with me to complain about the state of the place. And I'd also take twenty or thirty condoms that I collected each night, with a stick with a nail on the end, from near my fence. It was just like a parkie's stick that he uses to go around and pick litter up with!

I put all the condoms in an envelope and took them to the council. What are you going to do about all the prostitution around there? And what about all the rats on the spare land behind me? I said. The Council had the perfect solution, they said, 'We'll give you another year there, rent-free!' That will do for me, I thought, you've got to use your head sometimes! So my complaining - it worked in the sense that it helped me as far as I didn't have to pay any rent. But that was all!

After the caravan, I moved into this little office - my 'cave'. The 'cave' was as bare as owt, with just a desk, a little swivel chair and an out of date computer. After three or four months of being in there, before I started writing this book, I had the 'electrics' and the telephone put in and water put on. And I turned the back room - where the old wooden floorboards had given way and we'd put a sheet of plywood over the hole, into a 'bedsit'. Where the sink had been there was another big hole. And there was a toilet, which had been built on afterwards, which just went straight outside and down into the sewer. I used to sleep on a sofa bed. And it was so cold in there during November that Birds Eye would get in touch to see if I could store 5,000 turkeys for them, ready for the Christmas rush!

The lads used to come into work in the morning and pour hot water over me to thaw me out. I got some electric heaters in but I didn't believe in having heaters on. And even though I was two foot off the floor by then, at night I could still hear the rats running all over the place.

One night that massive fucking rat I told you about earlier woke me up. It was rooting about near my feet at the bottom of my bed. It must have been the brother of that other bastard that had been after my chocolate!

I set some traps. They weren't the conventional ones, they

17

were the big cage type traps. The rats would go in - but couldn't get out again - I've never seen rats as big as them. I caught three of the biggest - but I never got the one which had disturbed my night's sleep.

The walls and the windows were all cracked in the 'cave'. The wind blew in through the holes - and it was damp and mouldy. I'm not ashamed to admit that I wore the same clothes for weeks on end! I used to get a full, stripped wash in the little sink and look forward to Thursday night when I played five-a-side football and got my weekly shower.

I still had my pride. Pride before the fall you could call it. But I wasn't going to fall! I was 'reviewing the situation'.

But I was still in the 'cave'.

I was still in that derelict building...

That was the place where I was chasing a dream.

I'd been chasing a dream in business for the last two years.

'The Dream' is the fanatical sport's fan's retreat. It's that 'shed' at the bottom of the garden which when you open it up is your all-time favourite place. Your favourite team's changing room with hand painted shirts on the wall, a DVD player, a television, a drinks cabinet - and lots more.

Whilst we were pursuing 'The Dream' we were also trying to buy another business as an add-on, to get some revenue whilst chasing the dream. But I got 'double-dealed'. I'll tell you more about that later on. And I was left in this 'cave', this derelict building, with this big yard on my hands, with no 'get out' and nowhere to go. Everyone had left me. I sat in there at one of the lowest points of my entire life...

I'd started my business with only £1 in 1999. I was 'runner-up entrepreneur' in my first year and was in the final three of the 'Innovation of the Year' with 'The Dream'. But sitting in the 'cave', I'd lost everything around me and I had to lay five men off. I was in there on my own, the walls all cracking, the spiders' webs - I used to catch the flies and feed them to the spiders - just so I could keep the spider.

So there I was, taking important steps in my life, planning, 'the five p's'. I've always followed 'the five p's' - perfect planning prevents piss-pot performances!

I'd got pictures in my cave of the people I've met. People that I love and admire. Photos of my Mother, photos of my loved-ones - my son and my daughters - giving me inspiration just by looking at them. And my radio was on 24-7 - always tuned to Radio Humberside.

Basically camping in there had led me to go back in time and see what I'd achieved in life.

Reflection time!

Remembering where I'd come from? What I'd done? Where did it go right? Where did it go wrong?

How could I change it?

Which road did I go down? Cos we all take some wrong roads in life and I've been down a few wrong roads in my life.

But life's like a maze you know. You go down one road, hit the end - a dead-end - and you have to come back and try another. You go down another and have to come back and try again...

It was so cold in my 'cave' but I didn't feel the cold. Don't ask me how, I just never did and I never suffered any ailments in there either. I believe that was one of the most testing times of my whole life. And I'm sure you'll agree that's saying something when I tell you about some of the other problems I've had to contend with. But I spent two years in there from 2003 to 2005. I decided to write all of it down for my son, daughters and grandchildren.

In November, which is always a very quiet time for selling fencing and sheds, I started tapping away with one finger on this out of date PC. I thought what better way to offload these 'humps' off my back than to put it all down in words and show the world where I'm from, what I've achieved so far, where I want to go in life and how I'm going to get there. Because if someone with my background can do it and overcome what I've overcome - then I think anyone has a chance of doing the same!

At that time I most probably had little else to do. The game I was in was fence erecting - and pursuing my dream. But I had to just shelve my dream because it was a limited company.

We had five company directors/shareholders but I was told I couldn't carry on with the business until we resolved some internal politics. So I had to look at something I could do by myself. I'd been told that I could only be an employee, due to me losing my other business. I was advised I should put my shares into one of the other director's names - so I did. I put my shares into another director's name in fear of somebody coming to take my shares off me. I was led to believe that could happen if you owed them from your previous company. On his advice, I put my shares in my cousin's name. He used to be a managing director of three or four companies and he 'took me under his wing' - but then crushed me!

When I'd first heard of him only a little earlier and learned his name was Peter Hewitt, I was a little intrigued because they called my Mother, Hewitt. But when I rang him he was away on business. He later returned my call though and said,

'They called your mother Ada, didn't they?' I said yes.

'Then hello cousin,' he replied.

It was the first time I'd spoken to my cousin Peter. He was over fifty but I never knew he even existed until then! I got to know him and he advised me to wind-up my company, form another one - and put all the shares in his name.

I wanted to give a few shares to the people who'd helped me - the workers - but he said just give them 5%. And he had total control on paper of the business. I was naive. I was dictated to and I was like a puppet really. Like that Puppet On A String, I wasn't allowed to do what I wanted to do.

When we held our company meetings he used to say,

'Mally, in the eyes of the law, I own the business.'

The shares were in my cousin's name. And the only reason that I never had the shares in my name was that when the business went 'tits up' I got ripped off. My cousin advised me to put the shares in his name. I trusted him and I did...

The problem about the shares ultimately cost me a television appearance. The Dragon's Den is a BBC 2 programme for entrepreneurs. You have to pitch your idea, which in my case was my football sheds - 'The Dream' - to a panel of judges.

I had to present my company in front of five self made multi-millionaires on camera. You also ask for funding off them. I was going for £120,000.

I took a portfolio with me. I had a DVD and photographs of a prototype building that we'd produced and they absolutely loved it. They thought it was a 'goer' but I didn't get on the show because the company shares were not in my name.

I'm glad to say that once things had been sorted out, I did eventually get the shares back.

I'll tell you a lot more about my business dealings later on. And I think you might like that cos I've 'had my pants down' in business by people who I thought I could trust. There are some real rats out there and this 'pied piper' will name them all for you. It's a shame that we live in a world that the only person that you can trust is yourself!

I've only been in the 'business world' for a few years - and it's already opened my eyes!

Please don't get me wrong, I've also met some really nice people along the way. And met some true friends which without their help I wouldn't be where I am today.

They know who they are!

But back then I hit another brick wall.

My dream hadn't come true.

Everything seemed to go wrong around me!

I ended up living in the derelict building!

I was still in it when I started writing this book.

And I even had to sell my caravan!

See ya over the page, Mally...

CHAPTER TWO
KNOCK KNOCK
WHO'S THERE?

I was getting nowhere when I first started up in business. Nobody wanted to help me. Nobody wanted to open them doors. And that's when I got in touch with my local MP, Alan Johnson. Since then he's helped me big style. But back then I just thought I was getting nowhere in life! It provided another interesting chapter of my story however. It started when I was forty...

I was going nowhere but I desperately wanted to do something with my life. I'd never worked for anybody except the fishing industry. I used to have a little wagon. But to be honest I was basically still 'that man from the wilderness'.

I couldn't work in a factory. I couldn't work nine to five. I can't do anything like that. I always wanted to be my own man, my own boss. And I've usually had a little wagon where I used to go and collect a bit of scrap here and there, which I was sometimes given, sometimes not, do you know what I mean? But then even the price of scrap went right down. Then I saw this kid getting some of these big wooden pallets and he told me he was getting them free of charge. And I thought, not any more you're not!

I went to see Ricky Boyeson at East Yorkshire Glazing. He was a family friend, and they had hundreds of them. He just said, 'Take them away Mally.'

Gilbert Baitson, the local auctioneer also helped me with a yard. I was taking all my pallets there and stripping them. In the end there were half a dozen of us doing it. I was employing five people! I decided there's a little business here. We were building garden furniture and sheds out of the wood. I wanted to get the business off the ground, to expand it and make something of it, but I only had a pound in my pocket. Then I saw this programme one afternoon on telly - Prime Minister's Question Time.

KNOCK KNOCK WHO'S THERE?

It was William Hague talking to Tony Blair. He asked him, 'What's this Government going to do about the millions of pounds we lose because of benefit fraud?' And I stuck my hand up to that. Cos I was claiming my dole and still going out on my wagon. I was probably just 'pissing it up' at the time with no direction in life whatsoever until I 'saw the light'.

Tony Blair said, 'If there's anybody out there, irrespective of his or her colour, creed or background who has come up with a business idea, this Government will help them.'

I thought, right! I'm going to get on my bike. And I did, literally. I had a bike with no mudguards on. It was November time, wet and windy. Someone suggested I go to HABAC on Beverley Road. HABAC - that's the Hull Area Business Advice Centre - would tell me everything I wanted to know about starting my new business they said. So I pedalled down to HABAC on my mudguard-less bike and went in. There was a 'little girl' on the reception who immediately saw my bike.

'You can't bring your bike in here,' she said. 'You'll have to chain it up outside.' But I left it inside, next to John Bradshaw's bike, he was a business advisor.

I said I want to go into business! She asked me if I had a business plan? I didn't know what a business plan was, so I said no and I just wanted to speak to someone to see if I had a viable business. They said I could have a chat with this retired bank manager. Me and Bobby, my younger brother, went back for the appointment. Leave the talking to me Bobby, I said.

I'd got some photographs of the type of work we'd done, garden benches, gazebos, trellising etc. And I was sat there and I said I've no money but I've got this great idea of turning reclaimed timber into garden furniture and sheds.

Well unbeknown to me he'd already pressed a little button under his desk and two security men came dashing in.

'Come on lets be having you out of here,' they said.

What do you mean, I thought you were a government run business. I thought you were here to help people get started in business, I said.

'Yes we are but you need money to start off with.'

I thought we could get these 'business launching grants' and things like that, I said. And I refused to move.

MALLY - THE BOY WHO FLEW THROUGH WINDOWS

The next thing was that the head of the department, Alan Spears and Kevin O'Connor came down to talk to me. Kevin is a really nice guy, I've made good friends with him since. He turned round to me and said, 'We're going to put you on a little course. You'll learn all about gross and net profit, everything you need to know about starting up a business. Come back tomorrow and you can start the course immediately.'

So with my only £1, I went to 'Aubrey's' on Hessle Road and I bought some pencils and a writing pad. And the next day I went back with this little carrier-bag. There were twenty-four of us in this little room. I made sure I was near the tea machine cos I still didn't have any gas or electric at home. Cos I was doing everything by the book and wasn't robbing the dole. I was six months like that. I was on the bones of my arse. I sat next to this tea machine and this modern day bank manager came in and we had to write our name down on a card and then introduce ourself. I couldn't spell garden furniture, I definitely couldn't spell entrepreneur. So I just wrote on my card: MALLY - HULL'S NUMBER ONE!

I turned it round so the rest of the group could see it. Then we had to stand up and introduce ourselves to the other twenty-three. This little lass got up first and said,

'My name's Lisa and I want to open a shoe shop.'

I can't hear you over here love, I said.

'My name's Lisa,' she repeated much louder, 'And I want to open a shoe shop.' I thought I'd gone back to school, infants at that, do you know what I mean? There was another long-haired kid opposite me who wanted to open a hairdressers. 'And I want to earn £3-400 a week,' he said.

'What are you doing at the moment?' the guy at the front asked.

'Well I'm cutting my mates' hair in my Dad's garage.'

Well I had to interrupt. What? you want to earn 3-400 quid a week? And you're cutting your mates' hair at the moment, how much are you charging them?

'I'm doing it for nowt.' Well you want to cut your own hair, I said, you know what I mean, you look like a grease-ball!

I suspected he wasn't too happy to hear my assessment of him cos he stared at me and said, 'And who the fuck are you then?'

Why someone needs to tell you, I said. You're wasting your time. It's not going to work! If you're going to have a shop and you want to earn £3-400 a week that means at a fiver a cut you'd have to do ten cuts in a morning, that's fifty a week, ten more cuts in the afternoon, that's a hundred. You'd have to have a hundred friends every single week who need their hair cutting, to come in there, just to cover your wages, your shop and your overheads.

He was still glaring at me, 'Oh you're a clever twat, aren't you?' he said.

I said, Well it's obvious - I've just worked them figures out for you. Then I said to the guy at the front, Why don't you tell him? It won't work! He's wasting his time. But nobody did.

The next thing I knew it had got round to my turn.

My name's Mally Welburn, I said. I got all these pallets for nowt. I turn the wood into garden furniture and sheds like these - I showed them the photos - and I just need some premises so I can build up the business.

Then we had to do a little test. You'll know the type of thing... A bloke gets £10,000. He spends £6,000 setting up his business. He spends £1,000 on stock. During his first day of trading he earns £500 but 50% of that goes out on costs. There were lots of facts and figures about his first week's trading and you had to work out the answers. How much did he earn on his first day? How much did he earn on his second day? etc.

Within a couple of minutes I'd got it done and went to the front of the 'class'. As I handed in my sheet of answers, the guy in charge asked if I'd been on the course before because I'd got them all right. Whereas the others were still saying, 'Do you know the £10,000, did he pay that straight into the bank? Did he get interest rates? What happened about so and so?' They were all making it ten times as difficult as it actually was!

'Read what you see, just read what you see, all the information is there', the guy explained.

I need to be out of here, I told him.

'OK' he said, 'but make sure you come back this afternoon.'

I went across to the Hull Daily Mail offices on the opposite side of the road. I met Angus Young, a reporter who I know and I said there's something going on over there.

There's some sort of a scam. I was later told that they got

money for everybody they got sat in a chair.

I went back in the afternoon and all the class refused to sit with me. They said I was too loud and too disruptive. But none of them had got the 'nine-plus exam' right!

I stood in the middle but they said we don't want you in here - you're too disruptive!

So I stood there and said get me the man from up at the top, Alan Spears! Get him down here again. And get Kevin O'Connor down here again.

When they came down, I said get that bank manager out of here, he's refusing to work with me. Alan Spears said, 'Yes! you're a bit disruptive.'

I got everything right I said.

Kevin O'Connor took over the class and I said I'd like an apology off him, pointing at the guy who'd taken the group in the morning, cos I'd got it all right.

When I finally got back in the room the other twenty-three all had their heads bowed looking at their unfinished question papers. I couldn't believe they still hadn't finished. Then I went into my little corner and sat down.

Kevin O'Connor said,

'I'd just like to start the afternoon by saying there's only one person in here that is going to succeed after two years in business, because the facts say that after two years 99% of people who have started a new business could fail. There's only one person who has got the test right this morning and that's Mally in the corner. I'd like you all to give him a clap.'

I said, Fuck your claps, I'm off! And I just walked out, that was it. And I don't know of one of them that's still left in business today, I believe I'm the only one.

When I'd walked out at HABAC I started ringing the Houses of Parliament. I wanted to get hold of John Prescott - cos he was the Minister for The Environment at the time. But he kept saying to me you're in the wrong constituency. I didn't know what a constituency was but he insisted I was in the wrong one and he wasn't my MP and I should talk to Alan Johnson. So I tried to talk to him. I got through to his secretary, Jane Davis. She was really nice! She said,

'Well he has a surgery you know.'

I said I didn't know he was a doctor as well.

She said, 'No, he holds a surgery at the library.'

I said oh, is he a librarian as well? Cos I didn't know anything about all that politics stuff.

She said, 'But he won't be there for another two weeks.'

Well I couldn't wait that long. I'm coming tomorrow. I'm coming to the House Of Commons tomorrow to see Mr Johnson, I told her.

She said, 'You won't get in.'

But I said I need to see him and I'm telling you now I'm spending my dole money and I'm coming to London to see him. I was living with a girl called Belinda at the time because my house was getting done up. So I was staying at her house and I told her, I'm going to London tomorrow. I bought a return ticket to London, went to Downing Street, and got arrested outside number 10!

I had a 'tenner' in my pocket and a little tape with my business plan on it. It was a ten-minute video showing a pile of pallets and how I turned them into gazebos, arbour benches, chairs and fencing panels. All made from these reclaimed pallets.

I got picked up from outside of Downing Street and taken to a police station. This Chief Inspector with a peaked cap and a row of pips on his shoulder came out and said,

'We're arresting you for being in London for no apparent reason.'

Well, I said, I've got a good reason, I've come to see my MP, Alan Johnson.

He said, 'Oh yes, but he wasn't expecting you.'

I said, listen Sir, just have a look at my tape and my business plan. Fifteen minutes later he re-appeared and said,

'I've looked at your tape and I've been in touch with the House of Commons. We're going to drop you back at Downing Street, right opposite the Houses of Parliament, they're expecting you.' I said, get away!

And he wished me good luck on my quest...

The two coppers who'd picked me up dropped me back off at Downing Street. When we got there, there was a big photo-shoot going on in the corner and all the paparazzi milling about. And when they'd dispersed I saw Rula Lenska and Glenda Jackson. They were walking in my direction towards the Houses of Parliament.

I went up to them. There were two 'Italian stallions' behind them, and I said, Ladies, can you tell me the way to the entrance to the House Of Commons?

In a very posh voice, Glenda Jackson asked,

'Do you want St Stephen's entrance?'

I said yes, that's the one, that's where I've been sent to! And I added, And could I have the honour and the privilege and the pleasure of escorting you two ladies. And with Glenda Jackson on one arm and Rula Lenska on the other and the two 'Italian stallions' following behind we ran across the big dual carriageway and up to the Houses Of Parliament. Rula Lenska was absolutely gorgeous!

Glenda Jackson said to me, 'What are you doing in London?'

I said, I've come to see my MP, Glenda.

'Why have you come to London?' she asked.

Cos I can never get to see him in Hull! I said.

'What have you come to see him about?' she asked.

I want to get a new business off the ground!

'Why?' she asked.

I said cos I'm an ex-fisherman and I can't work in a factory.

'Why?' she asked again.

I said cos I've been down the wrong roads in life.

'Why?' she asked yet again.

Well all because of alcohol and that!

'Why?' she asked, that's all she seemed to be saying.

Oh Glenda, I said, Did you win an Oscar?

She said, 'Yes I did.'

I shouted, WHY???

Then I turned round and said to Rula Lenska that I thought she was a lovely lady - she's a Countess you know - and that it was a real pleasure to meet her. And I asked if she was still with Dennis even though I knew she wasn't.

Anyway they both wished me well on my quest as well.

I asked Glenda, How did I get into the House Of Commons - I think they have a secret doorway, don't they?

She asked if I'd been invited and when I said, No, she said, 'Oh dear, you won't get in then.'

I said I bet you a tenner I do. She laughed and said, 'You're on!'

When I got to St Stephen's entrance, there were all these

Japanese tourists waiting to get in for a guided tour. I knocked on the huge door. Knock Knock! It was a bit like those castle doors you see in Robin Hood. This little hatch slid open and a voice said, 'Who's there?'

I said, Mally Welburn from Hull.

'Hang on a minute,' the voice said.

Then I heard, clunk, clunk, clunk, clunk! All the bolts were being drawn back and the locks opened. It sounded just like going into our Trevor's house - I'll tell you about our Trevor later. Then the door swung back and the chap said, 'Good afternoon Sir, would you like to come in?'

I walked into this very grand corridor. It was absolutely fantastic. I had to go through this electronic scanning system. I'd taken a carrier-bag of yoghurts and a bunch of bananas with me and a brief case with no handle on it. And I was wearing a thick duffle coat, I must have looked like a 'streetie'. Then the chap said,

'Go through that electronic scanner, there's no talking, no smoking and no drinking at all when you're in here.' When I got through that he pointed down the corridor and said,

'Do you see those two men in white coats with that police officer?'

Well I could just make them out, they looked as if they were about half a mile away down this corridor.

He said, 'Go down there and they'll sort you out.'

I said, I'm not going to wake up in Russia with somebody touching my arse, am I mate?

'No Sir,' he said and repeated, 'They'll sort you out Sir.'

So I went down the corridor past all these huge marble statues. There was Paganini, Beethoven, Strauss - they were all there. And then these big crystal chandeliers, they reminded me of Charlie Pride, crystal chandeliers, and I walked and walked towards these two blokes in white jackets.

'Good afternoon Sir,' said the big one on the right.

I said, Good afternoon.

'Who have you come to see?' asked the small one on the left.

My MP, Alan Johnson, I replied.

'Just stay on those white lines Sir,' said the small one.

I've never been on the white lines yet mate, I said.

'Stay on the white lines and sign in there', he said pointing to a book on a table, 'And he'll come out to see you.'

Well he never did. I was in there for nearly eight hours and I never got to see him! But he did ring me up at about 9 o'clock and said, 'Mally, you need to get your train home.'

But before that there were people constantly buzzing about, up and down the corridor and Glenda Jackson went by.

You weren't allowed to talk, smoke or drink, remember. But as Glenda went by, I shouted as loud as I could, Now then Glenda! She looked round and said,

'Oh My God!' And just ran off!

Alan Johnson's secretary finally came out and explained,

'Look Mally, Mr Johnson's very, very busy. There's an emergency debate on at the moment, he's not going to be able to see you today but he will see you as soon as he gets the chance.'

I said I'm not moving. But I eventually did cos at half past nine I had to get on the tube to catch my last train home.

But the tube broke down and two coloured guys told everyone who was going to Kings Cross to get on two buses. They said 'We'll show you where Kings Cross is, you come with us.'

I thought they were from the SAS and were there to bump me off! I ran like fuck! And I found my own way to Kings Cross Station. But when I got there, there were no trains for Hull. Nowt for here. Nowt for there. Nothing! I went in the ticket office and asked how did I get a train to Hull?

He told me that the last one had already gone. I asked what I could do to get home and that I'd been on the tube that had broken down.

'You'll have to do what everyone else does, sleep on the station and get the first train home in the morning,' he said.

I thought fuck that, I'm not sleeping on no station. I've paid fucking eighty-odd pounds for this ticket.

'Well that's what you'll have to do,' he repeated.

Then this little porter who'd heard everything said,

'Listen, they've got to get you home. Get on that train to Doncaster, they've got to get you home.'

So I jumped over the barrier and ran towards the train which was just pulling out. There was a guy busking on the platform. He was singing Elvis songs, 'Well bless my soul, what's wrong with me?' He was doing his best, so I offered him the stuff out of my carrier-bag. I said there's some yoghurts and bananas here for you.

He said, 'I don't fucking want them.'

I said, You ungrateful bastard!

And I had to run after the train again but finally managed to clamber into the first carriage. There was all this red cloth and chandeliers and all like that and I looked up and thought, oh this must be first class.

There was a bloke sitting there who'd already drunk six cans of beer that he'd squashed and just left on the table. He looked up at me and said, 'I think you're in the wrong compartment.'

I said, And who the fuck are you?

'This is first class in here,' he mumbled. But by then the train was on its way. I asked him again, Who the fuck are you? And who are you to tell me I'm in the wrong compartment?

Well, all of a sudden the train's brakes screeched and the train started slowing down. The guy had pulled the communication cord! The little guard, with one leg shorter than the other, and two security guards came 'running' in.

'What's the problem?' he asked.

I've paid eighty odd quid here, I said. I've been stuck in the House Of Commons all afternoon. I haven't spoken for eight hours, never mind eaten. Then the tube broke down and I have to get the only train that's left. And then I get a half-pissed wanker like him telling me I'm in the wrong compartment!

The guard asked to have a look at my ticket and confirmed what we all knew that I was in the wrong carriage.

He put me in another one where there was about another hundred people with one spare seat. By the time I got out of that carriage I'd had them all singing and laughing and joking. They dropped me off at Doncaster, where there was a taxi waiting for me with a Pakistani driver to take me home. They'd arranged it all when I'd told them what had happened. When I got into his cab he turned round to me and said, 'Where to Sir?'

I said, To Hull please.

He said, 'Can you put down as though I'm taking you to Scarborough, and I'll get £250 because it's their policy to get you home if it's their mistake.'

I said, I can put down that I live in fucking Scotland if you like mate!

'No, Scarborough will be fine,' he replied.

When we finally pulled up at my girlfriend's house, it was about half past one in the morning. I went in. She was pretending to be asleep on the couch.

'Where have you been,' she asked.

I've been to London to see the Queen, I said, where do you think I've been?

She said, 'I don't believe you, I think you've been bagging off! Here's three black bin liners with all your gear in. I don't want to see you again!'

I couldn't be bothered to argue. I took my three black bin liners and went back to my half-decorated house with a little portable telly. I slept on the floor and left the telly on all night as I always do. And at 9 o'clock in the morning I heard...

'Have you been in prison? Are you trying to get a business off the ground? Are you finding the doors to opportunity continuously being slammed in your face? If so Kilroy would like to hear from you.'

I thought fucking hell! That's me! I thought I was dreaming!

I had no money left apart from a few one, two and ten pence pieces. I went to the phonebox and started banging the coins in. My name's Mally Welburn, I said.

'Thank you, you're through to the Kilroy show. Please give a brief description of why you'd like to appear on the programme,' a voice said.

Hi, my name's Mally Welburn, I come from Hull, I want to come on the show. I've been in prison, I've been down the wrong roads in life. I said it as quickly as I could but I'd only got as far as the wrong roads in life when I heard - bib! bib! bib! bib! bib!

I put some more money in and repeated my introduction even quicker than the first time. But I didn't get any further before the bibs interrupted me again! Needless to say I'd soon run out of money! What a fucking rip-off, I thought.

I had to walk over the fly-over to Maltby's pet shop. I'd known Pete for years and he let me use his phone. I got my message over to the Kilroy show first time.

I gave them all the information they'd asked for. My name's

Mally Welburn, I'm from Hull, I've been in prison, I'm trying to get a business off the ground, nobody's helping me - and I bet you don't help me either! But anyway I like you Mr Kilroy, bye! And I put the phone down...

I went back to work and continued stripping my pallets at the back of Gilbert Baitson's. But in the afternoon I got a phone-call and I'll never forget the girl's name, they called her Anoop!

'Is that Mally Welburn,' she said. 'This is Anoop from the Robert Kilroy Show.' I said yes, but then said you're fucking winding me up aren't you? and put the phone down. But then it rang again.

She said, 'Mally it's Anoop. I'm one of the researchers from the Kilroy Show. I said I didn't believe her, and put the phone down again. But she came back on again and said,

'Mally listen to this!'

I heard a tape playing in the background, Hello my name's Mally Welburn, I'm from Hull...

It was the call I'd made earlier in the day. I said I'm ever so sorry, Anoop, I thought it was someone winding me up.

'Mally, we'd love to have you on the show, can you come down next month?' she said.

I said of course. She asked if I'd like to talk on the programme. I said yes again, I'm not coming down there just to sit in the audience.

So she said, 'OK we'll put you on.' First she had to find out a bit more about me. I started by telling her that I'd been in prison. I told her everything...

I was after some land at the time but the Council wasn't helping me. So I got in touch and told them that I was going on the Kilroy Show and asked them again if they were going to help me with some land or not?

They said, 'Well, if you're going on the Kilroy show...'

I said I am, and asked, shall I tell them on national television that the Hull City Council are helping me?

This bloke said, 'Yes, tell them that we are, that's if you're going on television, Mally.'

I'm going on, don't worry about that I insisted. So it was all arranged. I was going on the Kilroy show. It was based around the question Should Mike Tyson be allowed to come back into

Great Britain with his criminal record and fight in this country? After all if you've got a criminal record you can't go to America. But a sportsman could come across here, six to eight weeks in advance to fight a 'no-hoper' who he could have fought on the airport tarmac. He was due to fight someone called Francis, if you check the records. He could have fought him and Bruno in the same day.

The debate was about - and the programme was asking - should people be given a second chance in life?

I'd been in prison for fighting, all drink related. My daughter Tammie and my girlfriend came on the show with me - Belinda and me used to break-up and make-up all the time. It was all very well arranged. We went to Kings Cross, went in a Daimler to Boreham Wood and were shown to the studio.

'Mally, can we put a little bit of make-up on you?' the producer asked.

You can put a dress on me if you like as long as I'm talking! I said.

'You're definitely talking,' he said, 'You're one of the last.'

'Don't interrupt Mally and don't be speaking out of turn or using any foul language.'

I said, I won't.

When we got to our seats in the studio I saw Kilroy standing in between two cameras. I clocked him, he clocked me back and I gave him the thumbs up.

And he gave me the finger, pointed back at me as if to say, 'Oh, I'm coming for you.'

Then all of a sudden the floor manager appeared. He said, 'What we are going to do is have an hour's recording. Robert's going to come on - we want you all to clap and cheer when he does.'

Robert then appeared and told us what was going to happen. 'We're going to start off here with the question should Mike Tyson be allowed to come into the country? These people are for him being allowed in,' he said, pointing to one section of the audience, 'And these people are against,' he said pointing to the opposite side.

'Should people be given a second chance in life?' he continued.

'I know someone killed your son. And I know someone ran your daughter down. And I know that you shot somebody. And

Mally, don't interfere, we'll be coming to you and your cue is,
Do people get a second chance when they come out of prison?
But please don't interfere,' he repeated.
I said, OK Mr Kilroy.
The show then started and it was a good debate about Mike
Tyson. Are people given a second chance in life? Kilroy then
came across to me and I ended up getting a good ten
minutes on air and we finished by laughing and joking with
each other. Should people be given a second chance in life?
The question was repeated over and over again.
There was a bloke in a wheelchair at the front, who asked why
should a convict be given a second chance in life when
people in wheelchairs aren't given a first chance? Well his
comment certainly started off a bit of heated discussion.
He turned round and said, 'I've advocated that we should get
more opportunities in life. I represent people with all types of
disabilities from arthritis to the severely handicapped.'
Well I've been diagnosed with arthritis and my daughter was
nudging me to speak up about it.
This bloke said, 'I've advocated that everyone, no matter what
colour or creed should be helped.'
And I stood up and said, Well you'll be able to help me then,
won't you? I've got rheumatoid arthritis!
Kilroy said, 'Answer that then.' But there was no reply.
Yes that's what it's like, I said. They don't want to help! And I
finished by saying there are also thousands of people like me
who have done a prison sentence and who want to do
something with their life but can't do anything because we're
not given the opportunity...
Afterwards we had tea and biscuits with Kilroy and shook his
hand and he said,
'You'll be back on again.' And ten months down the line, after
the Council had helped me with the piece of land, I was.
I was invited back and appeared on another 'Kilroy' - a 'Rags
To Riches' show.
I was in the last category. There were multi-millionaires on the
front row. People in the middle who were on their way up. And
some of us 'with potential' at the back. And the question was,
What have you done in the last eight months?
I now employ five people, Mr Kilroy, I said. And I have the

pleasure of paying tax and national insurance and all like that. I greatly enjoyed both of my 'Kilroy' shows. He was fantastic and very professional with everyone. And those appearances certainly opened a few more doors for me...

I'll tell you about some of them in the next chapter.
And how a setback ultimately led to success.
See you in three.
Mally

CHAPTER THREE
TAKE A CHANCE ON ME

My daughters were always telling me about Big Brother. They said, 'Go for it Dad, you'd be great on Big Brother - and you get three meals a day, a nice house to stay in and all that. You'd be away for over twelve weeks.'

Well, I'd never actually seen Big Brother, I wasn't into watching much television. But my oldest daughter, Tammie was very serious about it. She said I had a wasted talent. And even my youngest, Keelie agreed I'd be fantastic at it. And I think it was March 2003 that I decided to give Big Brother a try. I didn't have any money whatsoever, it was the end of the month, you know what it's like - money's too tight to mention! Simply Red! Oh, it's like the red box that led to 'Deal Or No Deal', £250,000 - and I had it in my box, didn't I? - I'll get to that later as well.

But with regards to Big Brother they were holding auditions in Newcastle. And I've got one suit, you know, it's always at the cleaners. But they're all right with me, they don't put it in the window, even though it's usually been in there for six months.

And I rang Big Brother up and they said it's an open audition, you'll have to queue up like everybody else! It was held at the Newcastle racecourse.

I had to borrow the money for a return train ticket from Hull to Newcastle, I think I changed at Leeds if I remember right. I then had to get a taxi from the rail station to the racecourse and I got there for about 1 o'clock.

And when I got there, there must have already been about 5,000 people waiting.

And I'm in there in my 'whistle and flute' - I remember it was thick snow. I had a bobble-hat on and a pair of gloves and I was queuing up with all these other people. They were all young and good looking, cameras were going up and down scanning the people in the queues. And I thought what have I let myself in for here? I didn't know what the score was, what the crack was. And I was getting nearer and nearer where we went in. They were only taking ten people at a time - into this old weighing room, where the jockeys used to be weighed. And every now and again I could hear a whistle in the background. A whistle, what was that about? I thought.

It was freezing cold. I couldn't wait for when we'd get a nice hot pot of tea! And when it finally came to going in with this group of ten, I'd got to know a couple of the people who was around me. And we went in this weighing room where there were cameras, producers and directors. There was this ten of us in a little semi-circle and this producer turned around and said he was sorry to have kept us waiting and all that.

He said 'You've got another six doors to get through by the end of the day to be successful. And what we'd like to do with you ten is we'd like you to dance like your Dad would if he was drunk at a wedding.'

Now if there was one thing that my Dad wasn't - it was a dancer! He was never, ever, a dancer!

But the producer said, 'Right we're going to start with number one'. I was number nine and I was already thinking - the chicken dance and Slade! You know from the seventies where you just banged your legs together, strutted around like a chicken and looked totally stupid! It got to the stage where number one came out and said my Dad dances a bit like this. Number two. Then number three - my Dad has only got one leg and when he dances he falls over. Number five said my Dad was born in the fifties and every time the music comes on he does the chicken dance. Well I thought, oh shit, what am I going to do now?

There was a camera pointed at me - and a big rod with a microphone on the end above my head. And a couple of gorgeous women in the background, I kept my eye on them! By that time I'd taken my overcoat off which I had on top of my suit. I took my gloves and my hat off. Then number eight came up. She said, 'My Dad is in a wheelchair, he doesn't dance.' So that was over quick.

Then it was my go. The camera swivelled round to me and the producer said, 'Your go!'

I just looked straight in the camera and said hey look, my name's Mally Welburn, I'm forty-five years of age, I'm from Hull, I'm one of eight brothers, first up - best dressed, and I've never seen my Dad dance, never! He was a big fisherman and he always insisted that we looked after our pets. My brother had a young tortoise but he couldn't look after it cos it kept running away, you know what I mean. And the tortoise disappeared. And allegedly we all thought my Dad had bit the tortoise's head off! You know what I mean. And when my Dad tries to dance he just sits on his chair, he doesn't dance, he just sticks his head out very, very slowly - then moves it back in again like this. And I did the movements to it as I explained it - very slowly and precisely. A little like Norman Collier but in my own style. I saw the producer was laughing. In fact by the end he was in stitches. And I thought, easy - a piece of piss!

After number ten had had his go, the producer tapped me on the shoulder and said, 'You, straight through to the next room. Everybody else, I'm sorry you've failed, but you,' - that meant me - 'you're through to the next round.'

I said, oh, what's happening now? And what they do is they give you a stamp on your hand and a little green sticker.

Then I was guided through to the next room. They take your photograph, I was given a number and you get processed. Then I went through to another room where they were playing twister and stuff like that. And by that time you were given a little folder with your details and photograph on the front. You had to fill in your details, your name, address and telephone number and so on and your contact details. I was told that I would be on film from then on and asked if I had any objections. I had to take the little folder with me wherever I went and they stamped it every time I got through another door and there were six doors to get through.

When I got through to the next room where they were playing twister, I was asked if I wanted to play. Yes I'll have a game I said, do you get a pot of tea as well? Because I hadn't had a cup of tea for over an hour. And I like a cup of tea. I leave the teabag in, not a lot of milk and two sugars.

They were all gorgeous people, only about 25 or 26, I was the oldest there.

I was then told to go straight through to the next room. And they said what we're going to do now is put you into groups of ten - I'd caught people up by this stage - and we then had to go into the diary room.

The idea of that was to go into the room, get 'miked-up' with a camera on you and you had one minute to sell yourself.

In I went. I sat in a chair and they put the camera on me and one of these gorgeous girls came and put a mike on me.

Then this voice from somewhere behind the camera, a bit like in Big Brother said, 'Are you all right there Mally?'

I replied I was.

'Right, then listen for a whistle, and when you hear the whistle you'll have one minute to tell us why we should put you on Big Brother. Another whistle will go after the minute is up.'

And I said, When's the whistle going to go? But nobody replied. I said, Are you there? And I went up to the camera and tapped on the lens and said, Hey, when's this whistle going to go? A voice said,

'Sit back in your chair and listen for the whistle.'

I said, Yes but when's it going to go? He just repeated,

'Listen for the whistle.'

So I was looking around, it was a bit like being in a bigger version of a photo booth. It was pitch black with a little light and the camera on me. And I was sat there looking at the camera thinking, what's going on here?

And I was waving my hand at it saying, Is anybody there? All of a sudden I heard this kid in the next booth going, 'Er, er, er, my name's er, Mark, and er, I'm from er, Geordieland, er. And er, I think er, I should be on Big Brother er, because of this, that and the other.'

I was listening to him when all of a sudden a woman's voice said, 'Mally.'

I said, Yes. And she said, 'The whistle's gone!'

I went oh shit. Anyway I was always late for the whistle at school, I said.

My name's Mally Welburn I'm forty-five years of age. I've been down the wrong roads in life. I've come through a lot of adversity. I think I can be an inspiration to others. And I think I should be on Big Brother cos my daughter said you get three meals a day!

With that another whistle went and the lights went on. I went oh shit again. I've missed out. But then one of the girls came in and said, 'Oh Mally you were one of the funniest.' I just put it down to my reactions. And without wishing to sound big-headed, after hearing some of the other contestants, I wasn't really surprised I got through. Then I went out of the room and they gave me my folder back.

A woman producer said, 'Listen for your name and when you hear it, step forward.'

She had all these files in front of her. There was ten of us. She threw nine files on the floor in front of her and then said a number, I can't remember for the life of me what it was, but she called my name out and I thought oh I must be going home, the others have got through. But then she said to me, 'Congratulations Mally you've got through to the final stage.'

I said oh good, do I get a pot of tea now?

'No, not at this moment in time,' she said.

The other nine all gave me a pat on the back - 'Good luck. Good luck. Good luck.'

So then I had to go in yet another room where there were even more questions and forms to fill in. They must have been as thick as a lawyer's briefcase. It took about another three hours to do it. And they literally wanted to know everything about you. A real far end of a fart! I remember one of the questions they asked was,

'Would you or have you ever had sex on television?'

Acting a little taken aback, I said could you repeat that question again?

'Would you or have you ever had sex on telly?'

I replied, No - cos I've only got a portable! And whatever I've got I have to share with my twin brother. And as I got dragged out by my feet first I don't think I'd perform sex on telly. That was the answer I gave.

They also wanted to know all about my childhood, my nickname? What? Do you really want to know my nickname? I don't think so!

You little black bastard.

What was life like at home? What? Do you really want to know that as well? I don't think so!

But I put it all down, everything they wanted to know.

MALLY - THE BOY WHO FLEW THROUGH WINDOWS

I'd been in children's homes. I'd been in borstal. I'd been in approved schools. My mother couldn't cope with us. That was the reason that we were sent away when we were young, because me mother couldn't cope.

The forms, the questions, the answers! It was never ending.

I put down on one form that I'd stopped drinking. I was trying to turn my life around. That I'd seen the light when I'd got to forty.

A little later, another woman came round, handed me a card and said, 'Here you are Mally, this is your appointment time for tomorrow.' I said, What?

She said, 'Yes, you're through to the next stage and that's tomorrow.' Well what does that mean? I asked.

'Well your appointment is at 11 o'clock - you'll find out everything you need to know there.'

Well are you going to put me up in a hotel, I inquired.

She said, 'Oh no, you're not at that stage yet!'

But I said what do I do? I've only got my train ticket and I've got to go home tonight on it.

She said, 'Well you'll have to get back again tomorrow if you want to get on Big Brother.'

I just went, Oh!

She said, 'Look, here's my telephone number, if you can't make it for 11 on Sunday morning give me a ring.'

It was already half past ten on Saturday night! I caught the last train back to Hull, it didn't get in until just after 2am.

There was a little fat guy on the station, in the booking office and I tapped on his window and asked what was the time of the first train back to Newcastle in the morning, please?

'The first train to Newcastle doesn't leave until twelve tomorrow lunchtime and doesn't get there until three o'clock.'

Hey, I said, That's no good - I'm up for Big Brother!

He said, 'You're not the fucking winner of Big Brother!'

I said, Hey, who you talking to? I could be the next winner!

'You could be,' he said, 'But we still wouldn't put a special train on for you. It will take you about three hours to get to Newcastle.'

I said, Don't you know who I am - and all that shit - you know how you do.

'Yes!' he said. 'You're the bloke who's catching the first train to

Newcastle - the bloke who won't get there until about three o'clock!'

So when I got home I rang the number that the woman at Big Brother had given me and it was an answering machine.

I said its Mally Welburn here, I came for an audition today, you've got me down for another one at 11 in the morning, but I've just finally got back to Hull, it's gone 2 o'clock.

I was at my daughter's. They were all very excited. They'd all stayed up to hear all about what had happened and wanted to know how I'd got on. I said, OK - but I'm not going back, I'm not going back again.

But my daughter said, 'Dad here's £100, get your arse up there! You've got a good chance of getting on TV!'

So I left a message and at nine in the morning I got a telephone call. They simply said we need you here, we'll wait until you get here. We've no more appointments after 2 o'clock but we'll wait for you if you can get here for about three.

OK then, I said, I'll come.

Well to cut a long story short. I got to the racecourse for about three o'clock. I booked in with the girl at the reception desk and I said, I was here yesterday, the name's Mally Welburn. And this girl said,

'Oh yes, they're waiting for you upstairs Mally. Go up to the diary room - where you were yesterday - you'll be in there for about half an hour.'

So I said, what up those stairs?

'Yes just go up those stairs,' she said.

I went straight up the stairs and at the top were two bouncers, a big coloured guy and an even bigger white guy.

'Where do you think you're going?' the coloured guy asked.

I was here yesterday lads and I've got another appointment - it's an audition for Big Brother, I explained.

He said, 'Hey listen, hundreds of people have tried that scam, where's your ID?'

I didn't know I needed any - all I had was a little appointment card but I'd forgotten that! I told them again that my name was Mally Welburn and the production team for 'Big Brother' were inside waiting for me.

'Listen,' they said, 'We're the security men on 'Big Brother' - we're the bouncers - if you went into 'Big Brother' and you tried to escape you'd have us to deal with.'

Hey listen lads, I'm only going in there for three square meals a day - and if there's a little bird in there that wants pegging, I'll peg her for you, do you know what I mean?

And they both looked at me, started to smile and said,

'Come on Mally, we've been waiting for you.'

I said, you bastards! They'd been testing me out!

I sat outside the diary room and the producer came out and told me the format.

'Look Mally, you'll be going in there for about half an hour. We'll ask you some questions about a few of the things on the application forms you filled in yesterday.'

It was a bit like going for a job.

It was a bigger diary room this time, with three voices behind the camera. Two and a half to three hours later I came out of there! They'd asked me everything!

'Mally we know you've stopped drinking, but what would you do if somebody got drunk and called you a black bastard?' a voice asked. Nothing really, I said.

'Yes, but what if somebody became very aggressive towards you?' the same voice said. Again nowt really, I'd back off, I replied.

'What do you mean you'd back off?' asked the voice.

Well, I'd be hoping your security men would be on stand-by for anything like that, I said.

What's this all about anyway? I asked.

'Well what if somebody offered to have a fight with you Mally?' the voice inquired.

I said, just a minute you're doing my head in here. And I think that's probably where they made their decision. I doubted that I'd be appearing on Big Brother after all!

But when I came out of there after more than three hours, I had to go into this other room.

There were two guys in there and they said,

'Mally, congratulations you've got through to the last five at Newcastle. What we will do now is submit this to London. The next thing that will happen is that you'll get a telephone call if they want you to come back again.' OK then, I said.

'You've signed all the confidentiality documents, don't tell anyone about this audition. You'll get a phone-call about two or three weeks before if you are wanted. We'll meet you at a secret location. Don't tell anyone about that either.'

OK I said again.

Time flew by but no call. Until one day I got this strange call off this woman, she said,

'Are you Mally Welburn?' I said, Yes.

She said, 'Would you like to meet us? We'd like to take you to a big house for the weekend.' Oh yes! I said.

'Good, can you meet us at the corner of Jameson Street, outside Fletchers, the bakers and delicatessen, next to the fountain in town?'

Both Fletchers and the fountain have long since gone from that corner I hasten to add.

Well when someone phoned me and said they wanted to meet at a secret location and take me to a big house, it could only mean one thing. I'd been chosen - it had to be 'Big Brother'. For the next few days, this woman kept ringing me up.

'Mally make sure you don't tell anyone about where you are meeting me.'

No I won't, I said. She asked if I had a suit. I said I had.

She said, 'Wear your suit and stand outside Fletchers at two o'clock on Saturday afternoon and we'll pick you up.'

I just kept thinking, Yes! I'm going to be on Big Brother.

So there I was, stood waiting at 2 o'clock outside Fletchers on a busy Saturday afternoon, when I got a call on my mobile.

'Mally, is that you standing outside Fletchers?'

Yes it's me.

'Right, to prove it's you I'm speaking to, could you hop on one leg?'

I was looking round for cameras, especially in the old building on the next corner, where Radio Humberside used to be, above the Post Office but I couldn't spot any.

'That's good - now hop on your other leg and wave your hands', the voice said. I did.

Then all of a sudden this group of lasses appeared on the next corner, laughing. I said I've spotted you. With that I thought I've been stitched up here and started to walk away.

And the littlest, ugliest 'pig' you've ever seen in your life came up and said, 'Mally, don't you fancy me? We've done this to ten blokes today and they've all fell for it but you've been the funniest.'

I said, I thought you were fucking 'Big Brother', you bastard! She said, 'Oh no, we do this every week. We wind people up, it's a great laugh! We find out who people are from local businesses and out of the phone book and ring them up. And we've had ten people here today.'

They'd got me from my advert in the local paper.

'Need new fencing? Ring Mally Welburn!' Well they did, didn't they? But I never heard anything from 'Big Brother', not a dickie bird.

My only 'call to stardom' had turned out to be from a group of north Hull lasses who were just having a bit of a laugh. And I'll admit I had a good laugh about it too - afterwards! But the story didn't finish there.

Over two years later, when I was going through a little shit patch, I got an email from a guy at Channel Four Television saying, Mally we think you'll be suitable for our new game-show called 'Deal Or No Deal'. And the rest as they say is... fifty-four grand!

What a life-changing day that turned out to be!

Little did I know I had the jackpot in my box.

The production team came round with a bag full of ping-pong balls with numbers on, each contestant picked one out and that's how they determined which box you got. A player is then chosen at random. I did fourteen shows and it was one of the best experiences I've had in my life. Three meals a day and all my clothes ironed.

Bit of make-up on and I got to meet the legend himself, Noel Edmonds. And it's become the biggest gameshow on national television.

All that came from the fact that Endemol, the production company who produce 'Big Brother', 'The Farm' and loads of other programmes, also make 'Deal or No Deal'.

And although I didn't get on Big Brother, they'd kept me on file. And whilst I was sleeping in that derelict building again, when I thought my dream had gone, my luck changed dramatically.

I still had the email address for Favourite Places, the company which marketed the dream, set up on the computer. They wanted the computer back. But I just had one last click on to see if there was any email for me.

There was one email saying: To Mally Welburn from Endemol. When I opened it, it simply said that there was a new game show starting and that they thought I'd be suitable to apply to appear on it. And to please ring this number. If I'd not switched the computer on for one last look, I'd have never got on 'Deal Or No Deal'.

But I rang the number, it was another answering machine.

I was invited to an audition for the programme in Leeds.

Shaz, a lad who shared the yard with me breaking cars up, took me. By co-incidence he was going to Leeds to see his accountant.

I checked up about the show on line and saw what the show was about. Twenty-two identical boxes and at the time it said the top prize you could win was £100,000 or a penny. When it hit the screens of course that had turned into £250,000!

On the web site they showed us the French version of the programme where there were twenty-two briefcases and you had to pick one. You then went to the front of the set and a banker bid for the briefcase instead of a box.

These production teams used to ring me up and talk to me and they usually seemed to like what they heard. But when I filled in the application forms I'd get to the part where it said: Have you ever been convicted of a crime? And have you ever served time? So I put, Yes, Yes, Yes - all spent.

When I went to the audition it was held at a hotel and I had to be there by 1 o'clock.

I got there for about half past twelve because I remember watching Sir Bobby Robson and he said never be late for an interview, a train waits for nobody! And that's always stuck with me and that's why I'm always early.

So I got to this hotel by half past twelve. The audition was on the second floor, so I whipped upstairs and there was five or six members of this production team there with all these application forms on the floor.

I'd been speaking to this lovely girl called Michelle, on and off for a week or so. As I walked in I asked a girl who was sitting by the door, Is this 'Deal Or No Deal'? She looked up and said, 'You must be Mally! I'm Michelle. You're a bit early, would you like to come back at 1 o'clock.'

I asked where should I go because I had no money. She said I'd just have to wait outside and come back at one.

When I got back, there were another forty-nine people already waiting in the reception area. They then called us all in and we were put into this 'holding' area with cameras on us.

The production team said what they'd do first was give us all a name badge and take our photograph.

Then we had a game of charades. We had a little hat and we had to go to the front and take a piece of paper and then act out what was written on the paper without saying a word.

I had to smile when I read mine - 'THE KARATE KID'

How ironic was that? It was the name we'd given my twin brother, Trevor, because of his strange antics when it came to the martial arts. All I did was slowly bow my head and somebody got it. I didn't get the chance to do any moves or anything.

Next we watched a film of the French version of 'Deal Or No Deal' and they kept stopping it and asking would we deal or carry on given a particular option.

Then they split us up into two groups. We played, 'Play Your Cards Right'. The cameras were on us all the time. And when it was my turn, Michelle, who was 'playing' the 'dolly dealer' said, 'Nobody's ever got to the end of the row!'

Well there's always a first, I replied.

My first card out was a seven. I was allowed to change it - and I got a ten. I went higher and got a King.

Then I went lower, from a Jack to a King! And I got an eight.

Then I went higher again and I got a ten.

Then I went lower and got a two.

Then higher and I got an Ace!

The end! I'd won!

She gave me a big kiss and a cuddle and we were all dancing around. I loved it!

We played more games, then they said everyone had to go out of the room and they called us back in six at a time.

The two cameras were still on. And we had one minute each to tell them why they should put us on 'Deal Or No Deal'.

Whilst we were all outside waiting for our turn to go back into the room I went over to Michelle. I asked her if a minute was all the time we had. I need more than a minute I insisted.

'Don't worry Mally, I'll interview you,' she replied.

When they called me in I had to stand in one corner in front of a camera.

It was like being at school. But I was as cocky as owt, I think you know me by now. She put a little name and number on me then said, 'Mally Welburn - action! Right then Mally,' she asked, 'If you won 50 pence, what would you do with it?'

I said I'd buy 50 pence worth of blackjacks or Mojos, if I'm allowed to say that. She said that I was.

She then asked, 'What would you do if you won £100,000?'

I said I'd plough it into 'my dream'.

She said, 'What's your dream?'

I replied, How long have we got?

She repeated, 'What's your dream?'

And thirty-five minutes later, after I'd told her all about living in the derelict building. And how the yard was haunted, how I'd been up and down like a pair of whore's drawers, how I'd been shafted left, right and centre by people who I thought I could trust, how I needed the money to get on with my plans, etc. etc! she said,

'Cut! I've nearly wet myself Mally. You're the best we've had today - you've rocked our world.'

I said, Oh fantastic - what does that mean?

'You're the best we've had, we'll be getting in touch with you.'

I've heard ducks fart before, I said.

A week went by and she rang me. She said:

'We're just working on the pilot, we are going to invite you on the show, I'll ring you again next week.'

Then she said,

'Mally we just need to check your criminal record.'

This is where I'd lost out before. So with a bit of trepidation I said, OK. I told her everything. How I was one of eight boys. All about my childhood! My problems! My time in the kids' homes! My time in prison! My boozing! My fighting! Everything! By the time I'd finished she was near to tears.

She said she'd ring me back again.

She checked it all out and she did ring me back. I'll never forget the first words she said, 'You're on.'

Shaz came with me. They paid our train fare, laid on all the transport and hotels. It was a fantastic experience. The programme was recorded in Bristol. We were picked up in a big limousine at Temple Meads station and taken to the hotel where we met six other people who'd also come down that day to appear on the show.

There were another twenty-two who were already down there who'd set the show up and done the pilots and all that. The following day we went to the studio and were shown how Deal Or No Deal was recorded.

Then we went into the green room.

You couldn't really get in with the original twenty-two contestants, some seemed to think of it as their show.

We recorded three shows a day. I met a lovely girl called Rita. She arrived with us and I 'clicked' with her and her partner Dave, immediately.

I did thirteen shows as a backing person. Needless to say the banter between me and Noel Edmonds was brilliant, we both absolutely loved it. I called him Norman a few times and I remember one day I told him to change his strides cos they were stuck up the crack of his arse!

There were twenty-two of us on stage and each of us got a box. You get the box by drawing a numbered ping-pong ball out of a bag.

After four days and three shows a day, obviously twelve of the original twenty-two had gone home. It was our job to welcome the new people into the flock so to speak, to put people at ease.

Then the day for me to play arrived. I did fourteen shows in all. My show was show twenty-two.

I'd never had a very high number in my box. But that day I had the £250,000!

There are twenty-two boxes with eleven red numbers ranging from £1000 to quarter of a million and eleven blue numbers ranging from 1p to £750.

I never had more than £5,000 in any of my boxes. I always wore blue and always had a low number. So I always helped the other contestants.

When it came to my go it was a total shock. I thought I'd upset a couple of people because I did tell a couple of contestants to go fuck themselves, so to speak.

One of them was a guy from Cornwall who was in the

original six with me.

He'd brought loads of Cornish pasties with him to eat and was always leering at the female contestants. Need I say more?

Sooner or later, everybody, no matter who you are, gets a go in the chair. I remember one girl called Lucy did fifty shows - and then only took home a fiver.

There's a big flashing screen and all the names come up and the computer picks one out at random.

At the beginning they'd asked me if I was available for six weeks. I turned round and said of course I am - if you want me I'm available for six months.

You also need five changes of clothing per day, they said. A day? I laughed, I haven't got five changes of clothing per year! They said don't worry we'll sort you out. I borrowed £100 and went shopping in the charity shops in Bristol. All the clothes you saw me in on the show were from charity shops.

When it came to my show I sensed I had the 'big boy', the £250,000 in my box. Then my name came up on the screen! The rest as they say is history.

The first round you have to pick five boxes. After you've selected those you get an offer from the banker. After that offer you pick the other boxes in sets of threes.

Nobody knows who the banker is. You all have your own ideas about who it could be. But you never meet him - even when you've been on.

I did have the quarter of a million in my box but when I got down to the last five boxes the banker offered me £54,000. I didn't want to take it. It took almost three hours to record the show. I kept saying what's going on Noel? And he kept calming me down. There were more outtakes than intakes!

Then I thought fifty-four grand! That was a life-changing sum for me!

I had five boxes left.

10p, £100, £250, £20,000 and £250,000!

My drop back was £20,000. But at that stage if I'd said No Deal, I'd have to have opened another three boxes. There were three blues and two reds. I know the odds were in my favour. And if I'd continued I'd have won a quarter of a million pounds.

But it's easy to say that in hindsight, isn't it? At that stage I thought it could easily have been 10p! And when someone was offering me fifty-four thousand pounds, well... Deal!

It couldn't have happened at a better time. It was just before Christmas. I 'sorted my daughters out' and paid the rates I owed the Council...

I met all the producers after the show and I've got photos with them and Noel.

The official adjudicator was a woman when I was on the show. And she sat in the audience and watched whilst we queued up and selected our boxes randomly by drawing ping-pong balls out of a bag...

While you're down there you get three meals a day and stay in a superb hotel. And whilst I was on site I stood in the queue with her and I said, you're the official adjudicator. She was a solicitor, a beautiful lady.

She said, 'Yes I am.'

I said I know how you do it. She said, 'How do I do it, then?'

I said it depends how you feel when you get up in the morning. If you're feeling blue you'll put the two hundred and fifty grand in number one box.

'How do you work that out?' she inquired. And you'll put the 1p in number 22. Then you might miss one and put the £100,000 in number 3.

'You keep guessing,' she said.

When I pulled the ball out for box 18 I had a feeling I'd got the £250,000. I just sensed it cos when I'd started, the first show I went on, I had box 18. And the show when I finished I had box 18. And I'd had number 18 five times in all. My mother died on the 18th. And the show before my last I'd had 18 - and there was a penny in that box. So when I picked it again in my last show, I thought - I've got it!

I thought it was either me or the people at either side of me and that's why I left them til last.

You weren't allowed to look at the audience, you had to keep your eyes on the floor manager.

Look into my eyes Mally, look into my eyes. They called him Greg, he was a great guy - and very funny.

So I had an idea that I had it or that it was very near me.

Nine times out of ten I could sense whether the east wing or the west wing had the money, the 'big boy'.

The adjudicator used to have a little book on her and when somebody pulled a certain ball out you could tell it was important by her body language. And I used to think it's over there. That's what I witnessed. And that's what I thought. It was my theory. I also used to have the theory that nobody would have the same number twice on successive shows - we'll probably never know if those theories were correct or not...

The grub was lovely. The hotel was lovely. You got the odd person complaining that the orange was a bit tepid or the water was a bit cold or there was no fried eggs in the morning for breakfast.

The only thing I didn't like was when the guy with the cornish pasties went into the toilets in the hotel and dropped his guts. He was going to blame me for it but I made sure everybody knew who the real culprit was!

The day after my appearance on 'Deal Or No Deal', Paul Hartley invited me on his show on Radio Humberside to talk about the experience. And people, some of who I didn't know from Adam, rang in to congratulate me on my win.

I didn't need much make-up on the show - I scrub up all right, I said. But for some reason I was soon back talking about the 'cornish pastie guy'. And I told everybody about him 'on-air'.

There was this one guy who came from Cornwall and he'd often break wind, do you know what I mean? I said.

When we were getting ready for the action and we were stood at our box, saying camera, camera, do your test, he'd come sneakily behind you wishing everyone the best. And then you'd hear the noise of him breaking wind and he'd say straight away,

'Oh, these floor boards are a bit creaky!'

Five minutes later when we're all stood there, with the two gorgeous girls, you've maybe seen Audrey and Karen next to me, no wonder I was sweating. Incidentally what a coincidence that was - the contestants at either side of me being called Karen and Audrey - the names of 'my first love' and her Mum - spooky or what?

But then all of a sudden they said, 'Mally have you just dropped one?'

No, it's not me, I said but I could smell what they were on

about. I like the smell of Cornish pasties and I knew it was the guy from Cornwall. He kept blaming me for farting but we'd sussed him out!

There were loads more lovely messages from listeners throughout the programme. One woman said that if I hadn't dealt when I did she would have had to have turned the telly off. She couldn't stand the tension any longer.

I agreed, I said when I watched it, because it was recorded well in advance of when the programme was ultimately shown, I was even frightened myself.

But I just saw the money. I saw the £250,000! And you know when you see it, it's like that big chocolate cake that we've all had. And we know that if we eat a whole one it can make us sick, can't it?

Cos it's rich and all that. And I think if I'd got the full cake plus the big cherry, it could have made me very sick, couldn't it?

I might have been in Amsterdam by now, getting three for the price of two! Absolutely agreed Paul.

'Mally's a great Hull lad and a great ambassador for the city - better than Prescott,' said another listener. Not sure about that last bit.

Paul said I appeared to be getting a bit of a fan club building up and the good part about it was that nearly all of my new fans were ladies.

One chap from Leeds emailed the radio programme to say how surprised he'd been by the way I looked. He'd only heard my manic voice on the radio before and no matter how he adjusted the TV 'I couldn't make him any better looking,' he joked. No, seriously he concluded, 'I take my hat off to him, he deserved his winnings - well done to him!'

You know what I've been through, Paul, don't you? I asked Paul. I've slept in that derelict building - for over three years of my life - I'm chasing that dream Paul. If you get that opportunity in life, you've got to take it! And enjoy it!

Many people had texted in congratulating me on my win on 'Deal Or No Deal.' The messages were flying in, from Nutty Nettie, Roz, etc. etc.

Keelie and Tammie, my two daughters, also got in touch with the show, congratulating me and saying they'd already made their 'Christmas lists' out.

Paul then made me blush by announcing that I'd donated £500 of my winnings to 'Children In Need' which was on that week. 'The Dream' is obviously going to be at the top of your list now?' asked Paul, this all still on live radio.

A lot of your listeners will know all about 'The Dream', I said. I planned to contact the F.A. and later promote it on every football club's web site.

But also Paul, I still do my fencing panels to keep young Flash and the other lads in work, so if any of the listeners want some panels, they're the cheapest in the town, I said. On my business card, I boast that I have 'the best erection service in the town.'

You've got to keep the bread and butter side going haven't you? And whilst we were advertising, I also told him that I'd nearly finished my book?

'You'd better get it finished whilst you're on a crest of a wave,' Paul suggested.

Even the lady who made the coffees, Leanne, passed on her congratulations.

'Did the banker know what you had in your box,' asked another listener, who was convinced he knew what was in my box, ie £250,000.

No I said, seriously it's all done randomly. I've been there for three weeks and seen it. When they come round with that bag of ping-pong balls, it's just luck or fate, call it what you like, as to what you end up with.

It was for me!

My songs, which I'd chosen to be played on Paul's show were: The Gambler by Kenny Rogers and Tubthumping by Chumbawamba. (I get knocked down, but I get up again!)

I asked him to play Chumbawamba first but I said I must say that I don't drink now, I haven't for the last seven years.

The song is all about how you get knocked down in life and how you get back up again.

We all go through ups and downs in our lives and you have to learn from it. And if you can go along through life putting a smile on people's faces - a bit of humour never hurt anyone - you can't go wrong, can you? At the end of the day, it's not all about money, is it?

And don't forget The Gambler, that's what I sang to Noel

Edmonds during the interval, I said.

After Paul's show we enjoyed a great night in Withernsea - turning on the Christmas lights.

But also on the Friday that I appeared on the Paul Hartley Show, one of my greatest heroes, George Best died...

That's it for Chapter Three, OK?
Some great memories there - and £54,000 from a
life-changing day that I'll never forget.
But as Jimmy Cricket would say,
And there's more...
And from that high I'm going to take you back as far as I can remember to where it all started for me. To when I was a five-year-old growing up in west Hull in the mid-sixties.
See ya in four.

CHAPTER FOUR
ONLY THE LONELY

In the beginning my 'home' was a little two up two down, terraced house, number 70 Brighton Street, off Hessle Road, in Hull. In the fifties and sixties, Hessle Road was still the heart of the fishing industry.

My father was a big man - feared by many a grown man. I'm sure they named that song after him, 'Big John, Big Bad John'. He was a mountain of a man and when he gave me that little clip around the ear - I soon learnt that 'bounce back ability' - usually off the walls! Then I had to stand up straight and stop crying. And there were times if I didn't stop crying, he would clip me again to see if it really did hurt. No wonder I'm a good goalkeeper. I think of the times when me Dad clipped me, and I just flew across that goal!

I realised just how huge my Dad was when we went to a circus in the mid-sixties - and 'the world's strongest man' was there. I was only about five or six at the time.

My old man had been a heavyweight boxing champion in his Navy days and what happened in that big-top showed how big and strong he still was. I'd say he was about six foot two inches tall and weighed about twenty stones.

At this circus they asked for a volunteer, they wanted a big, big guy to take part in the act. Well this strongman picked my Dad out. He laid him on this table, fastened this strap around my Dad's waist and put the other end around his own neck.

Then he started making all these grunting noises. He was really straining as he tried to lift my Dad off the table. He pulled and pulled but he could barely move the old man. And I think his fucking teeth fell out to be honest. But he couldn't lift my Dad.

In the end, after a lot more huffing and puffing I think he finally managed to get him about an inch off the table and then he quickly spun him round. But that's how heavy the old man was - he was a big, big man. But he wasn't a 'beast'. There wasn't an ounce of fat on him. Remember he was a chief engineer and before that he'd been a stoker, where he stoked the fire in the engine room, a coalman - the ship's stoker - he'd be shovelling coal into the fire all day long.

It was very rare I saw my Dad without his top off. In those days they always wore vests - he was always a big, fit looking man. He'd kept himself fit - you never saw him going for a run or anything like that - they didn't do that in them days. But his work at sea, shovelling coal and keeping the burners going was a constant 'workout' - non-stop physical work.

He was known as 'big, bad John' at sea. Even the skippers of his ships didn't dare tell him what to do.

My old man was a bastard to everyone, including my Mam. It wasn't her fault she couldn't look after eight lads. It wasn't my Mam's fault that she lost her only daughter in a fire.

Susan - she would have been the third oldest if she'd survived. I'm the seventh...

When Susan was killed in the fire, my Dad was away at sea. My brothers David, Raymond, Johnny were in the house with Susan and my Mother was next door. We had an old-fashioned fireguard, a metal guard with another piece of mesh across the top. It was an open fire, my Mum had to make it every morning, with a big fire blazing away. They were playing in the room, apparently Susan was playing with her doll. She threw it in the air and it landed on top of the fireguard. When she climbed up onto it, the top gave way and the frilly dress she had on caught fire. She was trapped between the fire and the guard. My mother was at a neighbour's house and by the time the lads went to get her it was too late.

There's still a photograph of Susan in the old man's front room. She was a lovely little girl. And my Dad blamed my old lady for it, for not being there. I don't think my Dad was a big drinker until then, but that really seemed to turn him into one. It drove him to the rum - and the whisky!

I don't know what effect it had on my elder brothers because I've never really talked to them about it. Whether Johnny and David will recall it. I know Raymond was only a baby at the time so I know he won't. There'll only be Johnny and David who will have any recollection of it. I reckon that would do anyone's head in, wouldn't it?

I believe that the loss of his only daughter was the turning point for my father. I think he blamed my mother, but she never deserved the beatings that we had to witness.

Some of them will stick with me till the day I die.

Believe me we lived in fear.

I can remember when me Dad clipped me round the ear and I flew through the window and woke up in the street. I was only five years old at the time!

Saying that what must it have been like losing your only daughter and trying for another girl?

And all you get is boys - another six of them!

And when my Mam was having twins after five lads, the odds would be for one of them to be a girl, you'd have thought! Well first born of the twins was me. Mally!

Not once up to this day has my father put his arms round me or showed any love whatsoever to me.

He did with my twin Trevor - he was his favourite. And he did with my youngest brother Bobby.

My Dad encouraged him in his sport, boxing, but I wasn't allowed to play football, rugby, cricket, or any sports.

Why I never knew.

I will talk more about my brothers as we go along, if that's OK with you. We all had nicknames off my Dad. Mine was, 'yer black bastard' get here! I'd then get another clip and be told to stop frowning! What the fuck's frowning, when you're only five years old?

He thought it was funny! Like fuck it was!

He'd ask you a question that you didn't know the answer to. Then - smack!

'Stop frowning!' he'd bawl.

Mother would try and stop him but she would get a beating in front of us and it all happened when he came home from sea.

A fisherman - and pissed-up!

We used to shit ourselves when he was due home.

Poor mother, we could hear her cries but couldn't do anything.

Mother passed away over fifteen years ago, God rest her soul.

The times we prayed to him, God that is, but to no avail.

He took the wrong one!

My mother was my Queen. There was only one Queen.

MALLY - THE BOY WHO FLEW THROUGH WINDOWS

I can remember sitting on my mother's knee when my Dad was away at sea. She would be putting a 'dick' comb through my hair. Then she'd tap the comb on a newspaper and we'd see the little dicks running around on the paper.

My mother was my Queen.

She had the gift of making you feel wanted. Loved!

She would put her hand gently over your face, just so she could 'read' your eyes. And what she told me has come true. Tell you about that later.

My Grandma, I only met her the once, she lived down Haverlock Street. That was my Dad's Mum, I never met any members of my Mum's side of the family until only recently. Until about two years ago I didn't know they existed. I was simply never told about them. I knew my Mum had a brother and he had two sons but they were always told to stay away from the Welburns. Don't mix with them! And they moved off the estate. My Dad has cousins, women, but we rarely saw them either....

I can remember the murder that took place down Brighton Street. The house was only two doors away from ours' on the same side of the street. There always seemed to be lots of parties at the house.

One night, a fisherman came home from sea. You could leave your doors open in them days. He went upstairs in the dark.

In the bed were the woman who owned the house and her female friend, who was staying the night. There was nothing 'going on'. The whole scene was a totally innocent one. But the fisherman stabbed the woman who lived down our street - I never found out why. You didn't find out things like that when you were only seven!

The story was on the front page of the Hull Daily Mail the following night. The trawler hand was only twenty-four. And the murdered woman only twenty-three!

It was a tragic but fortunately very rare thing to happen - which is probably why I remember it so well.

The murdered woman had three little girls. One of the daughters had gone in the bedroom and tried waking her Mum up. When she realised what had happened she ran over the road to Mrs Parker's for help. There was blood all over her hands and feet.

Mrs Parker, Vi, she's like a Nanna to me - and her daughter Eileen, who I recently found out used to change my nappies - told me that the fisherman had got home from sea a day before he was expected to.

He'd stabbed the woman over and over again, it was a frenzied attack, and he got a life sentence for the murder...

At the time I slept three in a bed with our Trevor and Bobby. Thank fuck the fisherman got the right house!

I also remember a strange bloke we called Mr Looney. We thought he was just a mad bastard, a bit of a misfit, but harmless. We were wrong!

One day he locked my twin brother, Trevor, in a wooden box and chucked him on the bonfire, then lit the fire! All we could hear was our kid's screams. Served him right! Our kid that is. He shouldn't have been looking through Mr Looney's window at his daughter rocking in her rocking chair and wearing no knickers. Our kid was unlucky. He got caught.

Cos I'd been there an hour earlier, looking through that window - and Mr Looney had chased me.

However I could run - very quickly! But he caught our kid. And chucked him on the bonfire and lit it! Honest, I'm not kidding. It's true!

Funny, I was the one who dragged him off the fire.

The locals called the site where the bonfire was, 'Foggy Fields'.

The very next night a gang of us was sat round the still-burning fire waiting for our potatoes to cook, as you do.

Well, you know what it's like when you're sat round a fire, the fire draws you in, doesn't it? You see things in the flames and you can be in a world of your own.

I was still only about seven or eight at the time, still living down Brighton Street. Dad away at sea - thank fuck!

I must just say, I love what I'm doing in life at the moment, writing my book. It gives me something enjoyable to do on these long, cold, dark nights. I might even get a web site later on - 'Mally's Story' - there's an idea!

Then I'll be able to keep you updated. And you'll be able to log on and send me your comments...

I'll have to look into that. Right, where were we?

Oh yeah, round the bonfire, waiting for breakfast, dinner and tea, all in one - the spuds! Eyes drawn into the fire, dreaming, not much has changed. All of a sudden everyone got up and ran screaming! Somebody shouted, 'Run Mally!' I didn't know that Mr Looney was only two yards behind me - with a big butcher's knife in his hand - whispering 'I'll kill you, you little black bastard!'

I thought I was dreaming. I thought it was me Dad, but I knew he was at sea. I thought it was the fire, the devil! Two yards away behind me, Mr Looney, the bloke who said he'd get me for looking through his window. The same guy who had chucked our kid in a box and threw him on the fire the night before. I looked round and there he was! This madman with the biggest chopper I've ever seen raised above his head, ready to strike.

Fuck that! I was up and gone like a bat out of hell! Never mind walking on water! I ran on fire! About forty foot of fire! I only had 'sannies' on me feet - and I lost them in the fire. Then when I went home with no shoes, my mother said,

'Wait till yer Dad gets home!'

He'd only bought them after his last trip - the last time he was home from sea - and he was due home again in a couple of days. My mother couldn't afford another pair, of course. She had to get his suit out of the pawn shop. My mother used to say the bloke in the pawnbroker's was the smallest bloke in the world - cos he could stand under his own balls!

Well, when the old man came home that trip, and during one of his many, shall we call them 'party nights'? - with what friends that me Dad had who'd drink with him in our house - me, Trevor and Bobby were the entertainment.

At that time my elder brothers were in children's homes and approved schools. I couldn't wait for my turn. To follow in their footsteps. And to get away from my old man and that mad bastard, Mr Looney. But his daughter used to tease us by not wearing no knickers. She was always flashing. And we would get the blame. But anyway - back to the party...

Daddy's home!

'Get down these stairs now!' he would scream.

By, you've never seen two eight year olds and a seven-year-old fly down them stairs! Cos last down got a clip!

Here we go again, happy as can be, my arse!

Dad was drinking Lambs Navy Rum, the devil. We had to stand to attention and then do our party piece.

I had to 'do' 'All Shook Up' by Elvis - or Blakey from 'On The Buses' - I hope they don't vote for me.

The winner got to drink about a quarter of a pint of rum in one go, in front of my Dad's mates.

Mother tried to stop him, but you didn't say no to my Dad.

Trevor did Stan Laurel and started crying, Bobby did Max Bygraves' 'You Need Hands.'

Well, I seemed to win it all the time.

Then the old man told me to, 'Go get them sannies,' what he bought for this big-footed twat. I started to frown.

And when I blabbed it out about walking on fire, he said, 'If you think you can walk on fire, I'll show you how to fly!'

Well I did fly round that room. I couldn't stop frowning - I didn't know I could fly. But saying that, I don't recall much pain. Maybe the rum was a welcome painkiller.

The times I wanted to kill my Dad. But when he went to bed he made sure we were locked in our bedroom.

Strange that I bare no grudge towards my Dad. Yes he is still alive but he is in pain now. None of my brothers go to see him. Maybe somebody up there is looking down. They say the Good Lord works in strange ways...

Maybe one of my prayers when I was a kid has been answered. It used to be party time every three weeks - and believe me it used to be my worst nightmare!

Them four words, 'Yer Dad's coming home!'

I had to go to school in no shoes, praying every night to join our Richard in that nice children's home in Sutton...

I don't know why my Dad disliked me more than my brothers. There's only one reason that I ever came up with and that was because of the colour of my skin. At that time I was darker than all my brothers. And I often heard the words, 'You're not mine you black bastard! You're not mine!'

It was so strange because I was one of twins, so how he came to that conclusion I'll never know. But the devil comes to people in mysterious guises doesn't he? And I think it came to him through the rum and the whisky! It always came out when he'd been on the booze. And not once to this day has he ever wrapped his arms around me and given me a cuddle. He's not once given any encouragement to me whatsoever. And he's not once given me any support, right up to the present day, not once!

Why? I don't know!

Maybe I was an ugly baby. Maybe he was hoping for a girl to replace the only daughter he'd lost. Then when he was expecting twins and the first one out was me - he must have thought, I don't want him!

Was it as simple as that?

Rejection!

I just don't know why but every time he spoke to me it always ended with my nickname, you black bastard. It didn't dawn on me when I was young. It didn't effect me.

It caused resentment later on but if that's what he wanted to call me, I'd answer to it. It saved him giving me a clip around the ear, didn't it?

I got my fair share of beatings even when I was young but I think my Mam was the main target most of the time.

There wasn't one occasion that he came home from sea and didn't beat my Mother up. Not one trip!

When the old man used to come home from sea you could smell him coming through the door. He'd got 'that' smell. He'd come home with what we called his 'sea bag'. It was like a holdall, about three-foot long with a zip across the top and with two handles, one on either side. And he'd have all his spare working clothes in it. But he didn't go out on the deck, so he didn't have to bring any wellington boots home, or any protective clothing, no waterproofs or anything like that.

All that he brought home was what he wore in the engine room. And you could smell that engine room as soon as he walked through that door.

Every time he got home from sea he would have 'bonded' stuff like cigarettes, whisky, chocolates and sweets with him. He'd leave his bag between the front door and the living room door at the foot of the stairs by the gas cupboard.

After he'd been home for about an hour or so, two or three of his friends would come round. You could hear the party getting going. We hadn't even met our Dad since he'd come home from sea yet. But if we dared, we'd sometimes creep down the stairs to see if he'd fetched any chocolates or boiled sweets back with him. And if we had the nerve we'd unzip his bag and have a look. If he was pissed-up he wouldn't know, the next morning, if there was a bar of chocolate missing or not, would he?

Go down, see what he's got - and pinch a bar of chocolate.

He who dares... You'd sometimes get away with it but nine times out of ten, he'd say,

'Who's been in my bag? And he'd find out - cos Trevor would tell him - yet Trevor had got half the chocolate bar!

Oh. Waltzing Matilda!

We were brought up on Patsy Cline, Roy Orbison and Connie Francis. Cos when my Dad came home from sea in the sixties, that was the music that he played. And it was played all night. When the old man was home you could tell what type of mood he was in by the type of music he played.

If he had Patsy Cline or Roy Orbison on, we knew he was in a good mood. If we got in from school and Patsy was on we knew everything was OK before we even knocked on the back door to get in. But if there was no music on - Oh dear!

I think we had a television from almost the time when they first came out. I can remember watching Doctor Who and wrestling. It was only a black and white television in those days of course - and you had to get up out of your seat and press the button to change the channel.

I was chosen to be the lucky one out of our family to pick eight from ten on Littlewoods Pools, by the way. And I did it for my Mam - and she won seventy quid! Eight from ten, I was only six but she won seventy quid - a fortune!

We used to have a moneylender called Sid Ashley, who came round every Saturday night.

He never came when my Dad was away at sea cos he knew he'd never get any money then!

Another programme I used to watch on telly was 'The Prisoner', but I never sussed that out. I think I might have been a bit young!

I also remember Sunday Night At The London Palladium. The old man was usually all right on a Sunday night. He'd sit and watch it and let us all sit on the floor. We weren't allowed to sit in the chairs - we had to sit on the floor.

His chair had about eight cushions and he'd sit there with his feet out, with his little coffee table beside him. At the other side of him was where he had his little tape recorder with all his tapes and that. It was streamlined, he knew where everything was, exactly where every tape was. We weren't allowed to touch them either of course.

The television was next to the door and he'd watch the telly by craning his neck and half turning round.

And it was when he went to turn the telly over that he 'got' you. He'd clip you round the back of your head, flick you into the room, so he'd got you trapped there. Then he'd stand blocking the door and you couldn't get out of that room if he didn't want you to.

When he stood like that in front of that door, he was a big, big mountain. It was dark! And he always used to say only get a sixty watt bulb.

We feared him.

We feared our own father more than anyone else in the world. That's a sad thing to say I know. But it was true!

Me Mam's chair was on the opposite side of the room. We were sometimes allowed to sit on that. But we didn't watch a lot of television. We weren't allowed to.

We weren't allowed in the house very often - not to just sit around - we were either in the garden or in bed or out. But when he was away at sea it was 'playtime!'

Then we didn't want to be sat in the house at all. We'd go to the ABC cinema in town - and try to sneak in to watch the films - on a big screen - and in colour! Or we'd hang around the bus station and try to pinch the box that they kept the money in on the buses.

Well we had to, to get some money for my Mam. But that wasn't the only way she got a bit of cash when my Dad was away. Every time he was at sea, my Mam would pawn his best suit. He was that big and the suit was that heavy, it used to take two of us to carry it to the pawnshop and get money for it. Then when he was due home she'd go get it out again.

Trevor, Bobby and me had our own problems when it came to clothes! We had to wear our older brothers' 'pass downs'. And if we were lucky sometimes one of the neighbours would give us a pair of trousers and me Mam would say straight away, 'Get them on.'

But then we'd look inside and see all sorts of marks, but we had to wear them! Going out anywhere, even to school, could be pretty embarrassing...

At Francis Askew School - that was my infant and junior school - I remember a teacher called Mr Blacksill, who was another big guy. And the French teacher, Mr Coiffe. He used to pull your sideboards, or at least at that age, the tufts of hair in front of your ears. That was his 'little thing'.

Mr Blacksill taught us how to play cricket. And I would say reading and writing and adding-up and all like that, I probably learned in my early days at Francis Askew.

I think I was very popular at school. My best friend was Terry Milner who taught me everything when I first started fishing. Another good mate was Ian Dobson, he ended up playing for Hull City and his Dad owned Gipsyville Tavern. There was also David Rowan. One time when I knew I was going to get a good beating from my Dad, I just 'legged it' out of the house and David's Mam and Dad took me in for one night only. They were really nice to me. I had a nice Radox bath, a nice meal and a nice bed with crisp, clean sheets. And then the next day the old man knocked on his door... Oohh!

The two Green twins, David and Lenny. When we played rugby with the two identical twins, I used to play loose man and David and Lenny were second rowers. They both wore khaki shorts with buckles on the sides. So when we packed down in the scrum I'd usually finish the game with a gash on each side of my head from these buckles. The times I've filled them two in for wearing them khaki shorts!

We were brought up with a family called the Cochrans. I always got on with young Jack. They called his Dad Jack as well, he was a black belt, sixth dan in karate - and everybody said he was the 'hardest' man on Gipsyville.

When me Dad was home from sea and later on when he was away at sea, me Mam wasn't allowed to go out of the house. And Mrs Cochran had a go at me Dad about it once. She came to our door and said,

'You beat your woman up, well try and beat me up.' And me Dad was a bit wary of Mrs Cochran cos he'd never had a confrontation with a woman who'd stood up to him before. And she really went after him - and me Dad shut the door, do you know what I mean, he wasn't getting involved.

But Jack never came round.

He wouldn't come and face me Dad. They'd have a drink together - and the talk was always about which one of them would be the hardest between Jack and me Dad. But we always wanted to know, if Jack could put you to sleep with just one finger on the side of your neck, why did he never come and put the old man to sleep for us?

Why didn't he ever come round?

But they were the family we got the closest to. And we're still all good friends today.

I'll have to stop for a break now but I can't wait to carry on.

I treat life now like a 'carry-on movie'. You have to laugh, and I'm catching up now on the laughs that I've missed out on in life. But may I stress, I think you need to be over the age of eighteen to read this story.

So please, just take me as you find me.

There's a load more to come...

But that's it for now.

My finger's gone numb!

See yer soon, Mally - the bounce-back kid!

CHAPTER FIVE
ROAD TO NOWHERE

I'm one of eight lads - there's a year between us - apart from my twin, Trevor and myself of course.

I was born thirty minutes before him on April 23 1958, St Georges' Day. I believe I'm your modern St George. Didn't he slay the dragon?

In life you're sometimes faced with them dragons. My main one as I said - was alcohol! What an arsehole I was. Right up to the age of forty. I thought I was that 'social outcast' until I saw the light. It's never too late to change.

I've never tasted hospital food. I was the one that tasted the prison food. Well if I could take that clip from my Dad and get back up again, there was never going to be any lads of my own age going to knock me down. Hundreds tried and hundreds failed!

I'm not proud of that fact. But it was either stand up and fight or lay down and be beaten. I became a target...

I can remember the first time I appeared in court. I was up for pinching milk and the money that people used to leave out on the doorstep for the milkman and the paperboy. But I used to take it and give it to me Mam.

Oh, I pinched a chicken as well. It was on the windowsill - just come out of the oven - by, it was nice!

I remember the Judge saying to my Mother that she was not fit to look after us. My Mother said we were not bad lads and that we ran errands for her. He said well this one, pointing at me, won't be doing any errands for you for a long while.

Well, my Mam started to cry. Then I started to cry. My Mam wasn't even allowed to give me a kiss goodbye.

My Mother was in tears and her last words to me were, 'Be good, I'll write to you.'

Heartbreaking that was, a sixth son being put away. I may be forty-eight now but I still shed a tear when I recall that day.

They said that the Judge didn't like fishermen or their families cos his wife ran off with one.

I'm not surprised - fishermen had more fun. They were the kings of the road for them three days they were at home. From a Jack to a King. I'll tell you about my own fishing days later. Do you know I can still smell that chicken...

From there I was sent to the children's home for the first time. I was only eleven. And I readily admit I was very, very scared! The home was down Saltshouse Road, near Sutton village, in Hull. It was a big, old house at the end of a long, gravel drive. It had a big fence around it.

Everything's big when you're only eleven.

Some of the teachers and carers were a bit strange. But call them teachers or carers, elders, whatever you like, I can't remember any of them, not a single person, by name! But I remember I could hear the cries of the other lads in there.

Mostly during the evening and at night.

'No Sir! Please! Please! No Sir!'

I must stress I never realised what was going on at the time. And I never saw what was going on. But I know it went on!

However who was going to believe a naughty eleven year old kid? Oh yes, I know it went on. And I'm sure you know what I'm talking about...

All I remember is that I just wanted to get out of there. Get away from those poor kids crying and screaming during the night for their mothers. And I really mean crying and screaming! And nine times out of ten it was,

'No Sir! Please, No Sir.' I could hear what was going on...

I think the thing that helped me was that my older brothers had been down the same path.

Our kid, Richard had been there and so had our Michael, David and Raymond. And the teachers dared not touch us because on one rare occasion me Dad went to the home, he ended up clouting one of the teachers. It was one of the few things I ever thanked my Dad for. Nobody dared touch me in them care homes. I didn't like it very much in there but it was better than being at home. Anything was better than being at home!

Oh you got the cane and that. And it was, Yes sir, no sir, three bags full sir. But the good thing about the home was that you got three meals a day! And they also kitted us out.

I had to wear big, baggy shorts that went down to my knees, ankle socks, with sandals in the summer and shoes in the winter. I can't recall wearing a tie but we had a little grey jumper with a blue rim round the collar.

We had to go to church on a Sunday and we all had to walk in twos down the road. Sutton Church wasn't far. After that we'd go for a long, two or three mile walk, then head back for Sunday dinner!

The only other thing I remember about the 'home' was that inside it was all dark wood. I can't even recall what it was like in the reception area. Our Richard recently told me it was a two-storey building and you could also go up some more stairs into the attic to play table tennis. But all I remember is the gravel driveway, the big house and the huge big gates at the front.

My Mam came to see me once whilst I was in there. But then I never saw her again whilst I was on 'my travels', except for the time she and my old man came to visit me in the hospital in York. But I can remember very little else...

As I say I spent a lot of time following in my elder brothers' footsteps. Our Richard and Michael had been in Sutton before they also went to Aycliffe. That was more like an assessment centre. It was in County Durham, miles away.

I was glad to leave Sutton Remand Home. I remember two other brothers that went down the same path as me in them early days. They were twins as well, Terry and Tony. And all they ever did was cry, cry, cry and cry!

They were really tiny and I used to stick up for them. I went through the system with them. Terry and Tony got shipped out to County Durham from Sutton, and shortly after I followed them. That was a bad time! Miles away from home, never knowing when you would see your mother again.

Mother always sent me a letter, as she'd promised she would - one every fortnight. But it was heartbreaking to read them, knowing what she was going through at home.

Trevor and Bobby never had the 'pleasure' of what I went through, if you can call it pleasure.

Life at Aycliffe in Durham got easier after four weeks of what they called 'induction'. That was a polite word for floor scrubbing, cleaning, running everywhere, marching - double quick, as well as lessons.

After the induction we were allocated to our 'house'.

I didn't have time to make many friends because fortunately I was only there for a few weeks.

It was a massive place, with hundreds of lads there. There were people from all over the country. The only two people I knew when I arrived there were the Munroes from Sutton.

I remember we played football on a pitch that was made of crushed house bricks. I didn't do many sliding tackles but saying that I always thought I was Gordon Banks, the England goalkeeper and legend, who I had the pleasure to meet a little later on in life. And I used to dive about on them bricks, ignoring the cuts and bruises I'd get. I just kept thinking about the clip off me Dad!

From Aycliffe in County Durham I was sent to Stockton On The Forest, near to York. And I believe they were the best days of my childhood.

My brothers, Richard and Michael had again 'paved the way' for me - and again that helped. And my Dad had also been there - for the Sports Day - and had clouted one of the teachers. More help!

I remember my first day at Stockton particularly well. I was made to scrub the toilets, naked. It was punishment for rubbing my dirty shoes on the curtains. The bloke that my Dad later clouted was the same man that stood over me while I was scrubbing the floors naked! But he knew not to touch - cos even though I was only eleven at the time - I would have hit him!

I soon settled down. Oh, Terry and Tony were there, still crying but you knew you were there until you were wanted back at home. But hey, I was happy getting my letters from my Mother. So for nearly three years of my life I was in that big house called Shipley House.

Mr Evans, the headmaster, used to get you in his office once a month and ask if you had one wish what would it be?

All the other cry-babies used to say I wish to go home. My wish was to stay there! I loved it!

The answer to the one wish was to wish for all your wishes to come true. I've always remembered that. But hey, be careful what you wish for, cos you just might get your wish!

They were very strict in Stockton. If you talked after meals you all paid the price.

On one November night someone talked at the tea table and the guy who made me scrub them floors had us all on the yard in our tee-shirts and shorts till that person owned up.

It was freezing. But nobody owned up!

If you moved, press-ups. If you cried - as Tony and Terry did, you stayed there until nobody moved or cried! But nobody owned up to talking at the table. We all stuck together.

Then I came up with an idea of how to get the lads into the warm house and out of the cold. That was to pretend to faint, which I did. The lads were told to go inside into the warmth.

Me, I was on the floor freezing! And that teacher, the same one that had me scrubbing floors on my first day, tosser, was kicking me to get me up. Well I knew I'd be in more trouble if I just got up, so I just laid there, motionless.

They sent for an ambulance.

Then they shone a torch in me eyes. I didn't know what to do next. Then they took me in the ambulance to York General. And unbeknown to me they'd got in touch with my Mam and Dad, he'd just got home from sea!

Lying in my hospital bed, I heard one doctor say to another, 'Do you remember the last case we had like this? We had to drill a hole in his head.'

Well, surprisingly I started to wake up almost immediately!

How strange! Fuck that! I didn't want anyone drilling a hole in my head. I was only eleven years old - just trying to get the other lads out of the cold and into the warmth!

They kept me in the hospital overnight, as they do, to 'keep an eye on you'. Well the next day when I was in the big playroom, riding one of them three-wheeled little bikes, I was five sizes too big for it, guess who walked in through the doors?

Yes, it was my Mum and Dad! And he gave me that clip around the ear and I flew off that bike and woke up two days later! So although I spent a day in York General, I never actually got to taste hospital food!

My Dad didn't just knock me out though, he also punched one of the teachers who was waiting to take me back to Stockton

Hall. He ended up in the next bed to me. It served me right, I suppose, but the teacher was a relief teacher who'd only been there a couple of weeks. He hadn't done anything wrong! It should have been the one who'd had me scrubbing floors, naked - and kicking me while I was on the floor, the evil bastard!

That was the last time I saw my Mam and Dad for the duration of my time whilst I was at Stockton Hall School. They say it's a mental home now for people like Mr Looney. Nowt much has changed then. But saying that, in those days it was just somewhere they sent you if your Mam couldn't cope...

There were only about sixty of us at Stockton Hall. I'd say there were only about fifteen of us in a class, and there were four classes. And they were proper classrooms with desks.

We had a different teacher for a different subject every day. We'd learn Maths one day for the full day. English - reading and writing - for a full day and so on.

Stockton Hall was a big old house in about four acres of land. There was a big drive down to the house. The headmaster's house was on the way down to the main Hall and there was a row of stables with a second floor above them which had a large clock on the outside wall. This was where they said the pink lady lived - a ghost! I never saw the ghost but some people witnessed seeing her. I used to shit myself just when people used to start talking about the pink lady. Behind the stables was another block of smaller houses where some of the other teachers lived. And further back still there was a paddock where one of the teachers used to keep a couple of horses.

On the left there were two new modern buildings. I was in Shipley House, the other one was Whiteman. And in between the two halls there was a single storey, glass fronted, dining-hall with a kitchen area. Each one had a yard adjacent to it with a big, brick wall around it. Further down, there were five or six classrooms - again single storey - and behind them the dense forest, with trees stretching away into the darkness. On the left was a concrete yard, about half the size of a football pitch where we used to play football with a tennis ball. We never had a full-sized ball to play with on the concrete. Further to the left there was a little pond and beyond that two full sized grass football pitches and a rugby pitch.

This was to be where I'd spend the next few years of my life. But what I learnt there was incredible. I wish I'd stayed there until the end of my schooldays. I had soccer trials for York City, I had trials at cricket, rugby, all because of the encouragement I got from the teachers at Stockton Hall.

You learnt things very intensely and if you didn't take it in during the time in the classroom you took it back to your 'house' to finish there, so to speak. You learnt more there because you weren't distracted. There were no lasses there for a start! It was all boys.

Discipline! Yes Sir, No Sir!

Running, fitness - you learnt the lot there.

The bedrooms at the Hall were like dormitories with eight beds in the room. They were all metal beds. On top of each bed was a mattress and on top of that we had a really thick plastic 'coating'. They were certainly uncomfortable, the most uncomfortable beds I've ever slept on.

Some of the other boys also had what we called 'piss sheets'. We made our own beds - we had like horse-hair blankets - but even in our thick pyjamas, they felt horrible and uncomfortable too. But the kids who were known as 'the piss-bed brigade' had sheets and a different blanket.

As well as the eight-bed dormitories, there were also two-bed and four-bed dormitories, and a single 'naughty boy's dormitory' at the end.

Whether that naughty boy was the boy, or the boy within the man who was looking after him, wasn't sometimes clear.

Maybe the man was a naughty old boy, if you know what I mean...

We also went to camps. Fucking hell, we went to camps all right, usually for the teachers' pleasure! We went to Rolston Camp near Hornsea. It was all little wooden huts, really old, I only went there the once!

Abseiling, climbing, cross-country running, walking, canoeing, etc. You name it, we did it there.

The period at Stockton Hall was like staying in a holiday home - once I got used to it.

Once I'd fitted in and got accustomed to it, I loved it.

Some people, all they did was cry for their Mums because they wanted to go home but once I'd adapted to it I didn't want to leave!

In spring and summer we were always involved in outdoor activities. We'd go play football, rugby, gymnastics - every day and every evening there was always something going on. We never just went back to our rooms and sat about. Table-tennis, volleyball, I loved volleyball and cricket - we did it all.

I can't remember any women at Sutton Remand Home and I can't recall any at Aycliffe either. And I can only remember two at Stockton Hall.

The first was the headmaster's wife Mrs Evans, she was really nice. She was the one that when we'd finished our dinners - we couldn't talk and we had to fold our arms near our ears - would ask, 'Does anyone want anymore?' And anyone who could get their elbows near their ears, 'cross-folded' got extra dinner. She was a lovely lady. And she'd say, 'Give it to Welburn.' And I'd go up and thank her and she'd say 'You be a good lad, young Welburn,' she was always really good to me.

She also doubled as our 'nurse' who looked after us when we were ill. We called her Matron. If anyone was ill and had to stay in bed she'd check on them during the day. She was a lovely woman. But apart from my short spell in hospital I was never ill. I never stayed in bed except the day after the Lyke Wake Walk when we were all allowed a lie-in, after our overnight exertions.

Then there was the cook, Mrs White. Every time you went to her she always put an extra dollop on for you. They were both very caring women.

But the first time I met lasses, females of my own age, was when I came back home at fifteen for my last year at senior school and into 'the flock'. But there was only one thing, I had no confidence, none at all, because of teenage spots, I was covered in them. I hated them...

The Hall was like a big mansion. It was a huge old house - a very grand old house. It had a big main entrance with two stairways, one for the staff and one for the lads. Two huge rooms, a boot room, toilets and a laundry room.

From what I can remember that was all on the ground floor.

The building was three floors high. And I recall that on the same floors as our dormitories, a teacher had like a flat which they lived in.

How they lived there, them teachers, with the smell of piss every morning, I'll never know. The boys who pissed the bed had to go in a different line to the lads who didn't piss the bed. I was always in the 'non-piss' line. But just like at Sutton, I still heard some of the lads cry out in the night.

'No Sir! Please, Please, No Sir!'

I just buried my head in the pillow and hoped to fuck that the 'bogey man' didn't come calling at my bed.

He never did come to mine but he went to some of the others! I remember we used to play a game called 'ghost hunt'. The hall was situated in about five acres of land and about an acre of that was what we called 'the forest', hence, Stockton on the Forest.

Well anyway in this 'ghost hunt', you were given ten minutes to go and hide. Then the 'bogey man' would come looking for you! Fuck that! I didn't want no 'bogey man' finding me and dragging me away into the bushes...

So while the other lads hid in them bushes and under fallen leaves, I would climb up the highest tree. It was dangerous but it was well worth the risk! Even at the top of the tree I could still hear the cries.

'No Sir! No Sir!'

I couldn't see anything. But I heard them time and time again! Nobody was going to get me while I was up that tree. I was always the last one to get caught.

One of the twins, Tony, was telling me only last year he'd been to a court case because a few of the boys pressed charges against one of the teachers, accusing him of sexual assault.

It was a very long court case apparently.

The teacher was eventually acquitted of all the charges against him except one. But what surprised me was that the bloke they were on about was someone who I always thought of as one of the good guys...

My brother Richard still remembers what went on but refuses to talk about it.

To me some of it was 'playground whispers'. But I used to see boys crying in the playground and asked them what was going on? And when some of the lads actually told me about what went on.

'You know what that bastard did to me last night?' or 'He was 'playing' with me again last night,' - you know what I mean? There was no reason to doubt that it actually went on, was there?

Everybody heard the screams and we all knew what they meant. Some of the lads witnessed things no child should ever see. Fortunately I never did. But we all knew what was happening in those locked rooms...

The best friends I ever met were at Stockton Hall. Paddy Tyman, Kevin Smith, Johnny Lister and Motty Milner, Terry's older brother - he was the strongest kid there, a weightlifter - he could lift anything! He should have been a champion.

There were more people with championship potential in Stockton Hall than anywhere else I knew. If they'd followed it through afterwards they'd have become successful professionals at virtually any sport you could mention. Football, rugby, cricket, tennis, volleyball, weightlifting, gymnastics, you name it.

The place was a training and sports camp in everything but name. It's what we need more of today for all these 'wayward' lads who have no focus in their lives. I met some great lads there, some of them I still keep in touch with today...

Not surprisingly the only thing that interested me at Stockton Hall was sport! I wasn't into maths and I couldn't write very well, you've only got to look at my writing now to see that! I still can't spell very well but I can add up. I'm good at Maths now. But then, Geography? No! - Art? No! - English? No! - all I wanted to do was sport, sport and more sport!

Being one of eight lads, and sometimes living only off scraps, I certainly liked the food we were given. I didn't mind that semolina or sago pudding, that everyone else used to hate, I used to love anything like that. I could never, ever leave food. I always had to eat my grub and I loved any food that was going. Meat was a treat wasn't it? And a bit of fish, mmmm!.... Yummy!

But my favourite was bakewell tarts, we used to get them sometimes on a Sunday. And Weetabix, but you always got porridge in a morning during the week and cornflakes or

Weetabix only on a Sunday. I suppose that's because they didn't want to give you milk every day for your cereals. They were little portions as well, we didn't get a lot.

I can't recall coming home once for Christmas in all the time I was away. Some of the lads did. I was never in Sutton Remand Home for Christmas, I'm only talking about Stockton Hall. You'd get presents from some of the teachers and it was just free and easy over the holiday period. You know, it wasn't the usual routine. All the rest of the time it was a strict routine. Some of the other lads went home for a fortnight for Christmas and New Year and then came back. But I think I only did that once. I think it was my first Christmas there. We got holidays and home leaves and things like that, but I never wanted to go home. Again I think I went home once, when I knew my Dad was away at sea.

We were allowed to go home for some weekends and come back on the Monday. I'd find out first, via the letters from my Mum whether my Dad would be away and if it was 'safe' to go home, so to speak. That's all I wanted to do, just go home to see my Mam...

Mr Hall guided us to the football final of all the schools in and around York. It was a buzz getting in that minibus to play our games away from home, so to speak - and we got to see girls! I was six-foot tall and took a size 12 in boots at the age of thirteen. I thought my feet grew an inch every year I got older. And I used to bite my toenails believing that would stop them growing. It never did! I was the only kid there that had to get their shoes made. I now get my shoes made by the local shipbuilders. My next pair's getting launched next week!

Well we got to the finals but we used to have to take a load of shit from them 'normal' school kids!

We used to turn up - and it was like 'One Flew Over The Cuckoo's Nest' and 'Kes' all in one!

There was one game, I don't know whether it was a final but all the school turned up to watch.

I was in goal. Both touchlines were full. I think the team we played against, all the school had turned up to see the 'skinheads' play. Oh, and I had just started to get me spots. Big spots! What a bastard!

Anyway these 'greebos' - long-haired wankers - were stood

behind my goal. And when the other team took a shot at my goal they kept trying to put me off by throwing things at me. You know, stones and pebbles and stuff, when the ref' wasn't watching. And when we were on the attack, one of these 'tossers' said he was going to kick my head in. I think he was just trying to put me off - which he did! He said he was going to do it when the game was over.

Well when half-time came, we were two-nil down. As I was going to join my team-mates in the middle of the pitch, this long-haired wanker came for me.

Well I put him on his arse. Then his mate came running up to boot me. Then while I was putting him on his arse his other mates came running onto the pitch and all jumped on me. Before I knew what was happening my team-mates, led from the front by Kev Smith and Paddy Tyman, ran to join in. I must stress I was the 'cock of the school', the hardest there, following in my brother's footsteps!

Well it was a full-scale punch-up. It was great!

Then the other team joined in. Then their crowd of supporters joined in as well. Then before you knew it all the lads from Stockton Hall all ran on in their Sunday best.

Well Mr Evans, the headmaster was among us. We called him twinkle toes, cos some people said he'd lost his toes in the war, so the story went. The mass brawl went on for what seemed like ages. Everyone was at it! When it all broke up, the greebos - the long-haired wankers - ran off!

I was dragged by the neck by that evil bastard, the one that had me scrubbing the floor naked. Well I just got out of his grip and turned on him. And I did to him what my father used to do to me! I punched him right in the face and he went down like a sack of spuds. That was when I knew I had that punch on me! He never picked on me again. I think he was too embarrassed to admit that a thirteen-year-old adolescent had put him on his arse.

Listen, if I could get up from one of my Dad's clips, I could take anybody on. There was no man bigger, stronger and more feared than my Dad!

That was a turning point for me. Don't fuck with me! I believe I came of age very quickly.

Whenever I knew I was going into a fight I thought of my Dad beating my Mother in front of us and not being able to do anything about it. I just thought of my Dad when I was knocking down kids who were three, then five and then six years older than me. It was easy. Punch first - ask questions later. Sometimes it was only one punch. That's when I got the label 'don't fuck with Mally Welburn'. I would fight anybody for a Mars bar!

Well anyway still in that mass punch-up in the middle of the pitch with that arsehole of a teacher flat out on his back and nearly every one of the lads in the fight 'accidentally falling over him'. It was deemed I couldn't possibly have given him all them cuts and bruises from one punch!

When the other team and their supporters backed off, shitting themselves, this old bloke came up to Mr Evans and the ref and told him how it all started. He saw those slime-balls teasing and throwing things at me.

The referee had no choice but to abandon the game. The outcome was a replay at our ground. They were not allowed any supporters at our place and we kicked their arses, 6-0! We kicked them as well, they wouldn't forget us in a hurry. But don't forget they had their Mams and Dads to go home to...

One of my other teachers, Jim Wilde, was a Leeds United fan. He took me to Elland Road and I got to meet the legend, my hero, Gordon Banks, the England goalkeeper! It was the 1971-2 season. Leeds United were on fire, Don Revie was in charge, and Billy Bremner, hotshot Peter Lorimer, Sniffer Clark and Norman Hunter were there. What a team - they were unbeatable! Well Leeds had just won the UEFA Cup so what a treat it was for me to go to see them play against Stoke City at Elland Road - with my hero playing in goal for Stoke. They got a beating about 5-0 but if it hadn't been for Gordon it could easily have been 10!

I'm like that in our five-a-side team now. If it weren't for me we wouldn't have got promotion this season. And I do believe at forty-eight years of age that there is no better goalkeeper in this town at my age. And for that I thank Mr Hall from Stockton Hall.

I also won the golden gloves for the best goalkeeper not just in our league but in all three leagues that play five-a-side on a Thursday night at the Vulcan Centre in Hull.

MALLY - THE BOY WHO FLEW THROUGH WINDOWS

The Vulcan Centre is a new indoor sports centre built on the same site as Hull City's new stadium. They call it the KC - it's great. I believe that 'City' are going in the right direction. I believe Adam Pearson, the City Chairman and the team he has got with him including his management team led by Peter Taylor and the players he's got, are good enough to get Hull City to where he wants them to be. I think Adam Pearson has got vision. I like him. He's a good businessman and the town should back him all the way, he knows what he's doing...

I had trials for Hull City when I was fifteen. It was when fat Fred Smith was there. I got through to the last fifteen out of about 200 - and that was as a striker! Nobody dared come near this big lad - the big clumsy bastard up front - I just knocked them out of the way. It was easy. Ask Ian Dobson, he got to play full time for Hull City! It was my dream but I wasn't allowed to go training when my Dad was home from sea! But when I was in approved school they let us fulfil our dreams. And if we were into sport they pushed us all the way. Mr Hall was that guy. He was an ex-professional and he taught me the skills of being a goalkeeper. He was one of the really good guys. Saying that I only came across that one nasty guy - the one that had me scrubbing the floors, naked.

There were only about sixty kids in Stockton Hall and we had some gifted young, fit footballers. I'm sure that if some of them had kept it up they could have made it professionally. I believe I could have made it, but as I've said my Dad never gave me the slightest bit of encouragement. He never pushed me - even when I got out of approved school at the age of fifteen - apart from the clip around the ear.

My Dad just told me to get a 'proper job' so I ended up going deep sea trawling for about fifteen years. What a fucking waste of my life that was! Anyway I'll tell you about that later on, we're still at Stockton Hall and I've been treated to go and see Leeds play Stoke...

At that early age of eleven all I wanted to be was Gordon Banks, who won the World Cup with England in 1966. It broke my heart when he lost his eye in a car accident. And that save from Pele!

Unfortunately Leeds pissed all over Stoke that night, I was in tears. But then, just when I thought we were heading back to school, we took a short cut through the stadium. It led us straight to Don Revie's office, where I not only met the great man himself, Don Revie, I also met most of the Leeds players. But the biggest surprise was when the 'one and only' walked through the door. Yes it was the man that had made the best save in the world from the best player in the world, Pele. It was my hero, Gordon Banks.

I spoke to Gordon and got his autograph. I had a picture of his legendary save against Pele which I'd cut out of a comic. And when I knew I was going to see Stoke play, I'd made sure I remembered to take it with me, hoping but never really believing, that I might get the chance to meet my hero.

I can't describe how I felt as I watched him sign it. It was just like meeting Elvis Presley, meeting my all time hero. I can't remember exactly what I asked Gordon, I was probably too overcome and dumb-struck. It was a total shock for me that meeting. Jim had a camera with him and he took some photographs of me and Gordon - together! And a week or so later, he sent one of them home for my Mam and Dad to keep. Me Mam put it on the mantelpiece but when the old man came home he thought it was me and me Mam's boyfriend and gave her a good hiding! The bastard! Even when I got something that I could treasure, he went and spoiled it!

I was as big as I am today when I was a teenager and also easily the best goalkeeper at the Hall. I had trials for York City whilst there, and I had trials with Hull City when I came home, when my Dad was away at sea.

I remember I played my trial games in my bare feet by the way, cos I didn't yet have any boots big enough to fit me. But me Granddad, 'Pops' they called him, spragged on me to me Dad that I'd been playing. Nothing changed...

But that day at Elland Road was a day I'll never forget.

Another day that I'll never forget is when I met another of my all time favourite legends, Sir Bobby Robson.

But again that's something for later...

Another of my 'sporting triumphs' at Stockton Hall was when I completed the famous Lyke Wake Walk. That's a forty-two mile walk across the Yorkshire Moors from Osmotherly to Ravenscar. By that was spooky cos we did it during the night! I was fourteen. And I think we slept for two whole days after that trek. We got a badge in the shape of a coffin. They say the Monks used to carry the dead across the Moors, that's why we got that coffin badge. You might as well be dead after that walk. It makes you wonder how they ever did it doesn't it? Well, I've walked that walk. I also walked the 'three peaks'. The peaks are named Penyghent, Whernside and Inglebrough and that walk is twenty-odd miles. It's funny but I always remember all those strange names.

It could well be due to the fact that I completed both the Lyke Wake Walk and the Three Peaks in cricket boots. Yes! cricket boots. Well I was taking a size thirteen by then. So biting your toenails definitely doesn't stop your feet growing. And I had an in-growing toenail as well. And my face was full of spots, I mean full-blown acne, spotty, spotty face Welburn at that.

I was due to go back into the wilderness to join my twin and younger brother, Bobby.

Yes I was going home - but that was not my home! I had never grown up with Trevor and Bobby and my Dad had stopped going to sea. Fuck me, I was going home to that!

How could I adjust to join that rat race I was going home to? Why did I have to leave Stockton Hall, which I thought was my home. They taught me loads. We lived for sport. They pushed you all the way. I owe that school a lot, as you"ll find out. Because the next chapter is all about being that outcast. Picture it.

Being away from the flock for nearly four years and returning to it, twice as strong as any other lad my age.

Being away from the community. Standing out like a sore thumb, full of spots, what a nightmare.

Having a fight every day because they all wanted to fight the 'outcast'. And how they all fell by the wayside when they tried. All that's in chapter six OK.

Oh, that's also the time I slept in a shelter on the docks and made my first trip to sea.

So I'll see you in six, see ya!

CHAPTER SIX
TEENAGE RAMPAGE

Can I just say before we start this chapter about my teenage years, that they're also the start of my aggressive years. So please be aware that there are a few more swear words because while I'm typing, it just all comes back and I feel as though I'm back living it all over again. I don't mean to offend anyone but that's just the way it was.

Also you will notice that my pet nickname off my Dad, 'You black bastard' will crop up every now and again.

I need to tell you I'm not black, I'm just dark skinned. I was the darkest of all my brothers, hence the nickname, OK.

Well, here we go. I hope you have a nice pot of tea by your side, or something a little stronger if that's what you prefer, I don't anymore of course, so sit back and relax...

Well, the day finally came when Mr Evans, the headmaster of Stockton Hall, invited me into his office.

He told me I'd be leaving at the end of the month. It was time for me to go out into that big, wide world and spend my last school year with my twin and younger brother.

The school that was chosen for me was called Kingston High School, off Pickering Road, in Hull.

Well, having to leave Stockton Hall really broke my heart because I was down to have more trials for York City as a goalkeeper. And I knew I had no chance of fulfilling my dream at my so called 'home' in Hull because my Dad was home from sea, working on the tugs. That was a daytime job, he was at home every night. I just kept getting flashbacks of the last time I was at home and the last time I met my Dad in York hospital.

I had sleepless nights them last few weeks at Stockton and I joined the 'pissing the bed' gang. I'm not sure, I might even have shit the bed on the last night.

I did think of running away from Stockton, but why run away

from the only place you called home.

I really was dreading going home, well, what I called home.

At our final assembly at Stockton we had to stand in front of all the school and sing, 'God be with you till we meet again'. We also read something from the good Lord's book. I chose for those in peril on the sea.

I was devastated to leave that school. I don't know who took me to York train station. But I remember that there was nobody to meet me at the other end in Hull. I had to find my own way to our house at number 11, West Grove, Gipsyville. When I think of it now, it always reminds me of the old joke about the uncaring parents who'd moved house whilst the kid was out and 'forgot' to tell him where they'd moved to! I'm sure you'll know the one I mean. Well that was me!

I was dreading going home.

Can you picture it - me joining 'the flock' again after all the time I'd been away? I knew nobody, not even my own brothers. And on top of that at fourteen I was six-foot tall and built like that brick shithouse. Oh, and full of fucking acne. I'd not been in a class with girls since I was about eight years of age. I knew my new school was going to be a nightmare!

Well, I walked through the front door of number 11 without knocking. It wasn't a 'home' so if it's OK with you we'll call the place where I lived, 'Number 11'.

My Father who hadn't changed leapt from his chair, screaming, 'Use the fucking back door, you black bastard. And wait till I call you in.'

What a welcome. What a homecoming!

Oh! What the fuck was I doing there?

I had to go out the front door and go round the back way.

There, pulling up weeds in the garden was my twin Trevor and my younger brother, Bobby.

They didn't seem to recognise me at first. Was it the spots? By they were bad. I must stress I have lovely skin now.

I tried all sorts to get rid of those spots. Even pissing in my hands and rubbing the piss into my face. Someone told me that would help but it was only an old wife's tale.

Fuck that being a piss-head.

But saying that I ended up being a real 'piss-head', literally.

Tell you more about that as we go along.

The garden was a mass of sheds. It looked like a shanty town.
I was soon to find out what was in them sheds!

The house has not changed to this day, so they tell me.

Anyway even when Trevor and Bobby realised who I was they
dared not talk to me cos they knew my Dad was
watching us all through the window.

You know we had them net curtains that you could see out
from in the house but you couldn't see in through them from
outside - not like Mr Looney's!

They eventually looked up and mumbled in a very sad tone,
'Hi, welcome home.'

Well anyway, there I was knocking at the back door of my own
house - my loving home - on my first day home from approved
school. What a welcome! But there was no reply. Knock!
Knock! Knock!

I thought my old man had gone deaf in his old age. So I
banged louder. Then I heard,

'Come on in!' Well that was it! I'll never forget the words he
greeted me with,

'Who the fuck do you think you are, banging like that? Now
get up them stairs and get out of them clothes and get them
rags on! You can save them clothes for school. And then get in
the garden and help them bastards out there, till I tell you to
come in.'

I could already sense this was not my home. But as I walked
through the living room door there was the love of my life, my
Mother. But she wasn't the Mother I knew! She wasn't the
same person I remembered and had looked forward to seeing
again all that time!

Mother had an illness, where she hardly recognised me. My
poor Mam, all she did was talk to herself.

I'm not surprised living with 'big, bad John who was still that
giant of a man. But she wasn't the mother I knew. She'd just
go and stand in a corner and mumble to herself.

She'd go through that stage for six or seven months. She'd be
talking to herself and then all of a sudden she'd just burst out
laughing. She wouldn't know where she was, God bless her.
She got so confused.

She had this 'thing' about butter. She'd open the tub of butter,
dip her fingers in, eat the butter, then put the lid back on and

put the tub back on the shelf.

But you couldn't even have a conversation with her. She just wasn't with it. You couldn't communicate with her at all. One minute you'd be sat there and she'd start laughing, start talking to herself or breaking down.

On one occasion she got caught in Jacksons pinching butter. Not actually pinching it, just eating it. But they locked her in the back. We found out - me and me three brothers - and we went and just barged in there.

I think I clouted the manager, You know what I mean, don't lock my mother up!

She didn't even know where she was. She was just a total wreck - a total bag of nerves. She'd lost loads of weight. She loved her hair. She had lovely auburn hair and all she ever wanted when I came home from sea was to see me. And that's the only reason I ever went back there - to see my Mam and to take her a little treat. I'd buy her some hair spray or some cigs or I'd get her some stockings. It was no good giving her money, me old man would have taken it off her. He sometimes took the cigs off her but he was bald so he wouldn't take the hairspray - and I don't know about wearing the stockings!

They say she was the most beautiful woman on Hessle Road in her prime. And in her younger days, everybody was after my Mam. Everybody - even my Dad's brothers - I think that's where the fighting came in!

There wasn't much difference between me Mam and Dad's ages, about three or four years?

My Mam was the most beautiful woman on Hessle Road and apparently me Dad was the best looking man...

My Mam took me upstairs and showed me the bedroom that I was to share with Trevor and Bobby. We had our own beds and there was a chest of drawers for what few clothes we had.

My Mam gave me a big hug and lots of kisses and said, 'Take no notice of your Dad. He has just lost his job and he doesn't like working on them tugs. But he will be going away again soon.'

My Mother was a bag of nerves. It broke my heart to see the state she was in but what could I do?

The old man laid the house rules down.

We had to ask to play out. We had to ask to go to bed. We even had to ask to go to the toilet!

We weren't allowed to play any sports. And we had to ask to come into the house and then had to stand to attention when we'd been allowed in. Fuck me! It was like the house of horrors when the old man was home!

What the fuck had I come back to? And I hadn't even been to my new school yet!

Well I joined my brothers in the garden after the old man had laid the rules down finishing off with, 'You spotty faced black bastard, now get in that garden. What a welcome home that was!

Trevor and Bobby were shit scared of me Dad. Nightmare on Gipsyville - and that was just living at 'Number 11'!

Well my first day at Kingston High School duly arrived. I went with our Trevor and Bobby. I had to wear the sports blazer which I'd come home from approved school with. Dad didn't believe in school uniforms.

He said you went to school to learn, not to show other people how you dressed, he might have had a point nowadays.

But you had to wear the school uniform.

However my Dad just said, 'Tell them that I sent you like that!' He might as well have named me Sue! You know that song, 'A Boy Named Sue' by Johnny Cash.

Everyone was in school uniform apart from me and our kid. Talk about sticking out like two sore thumbs!

On the way to school I could see everyone staring at me as though I was that freak that had just rolled into town.

Our kid, Trevor was telling me about the school bully who was the hardcase of the school.

He'd beaten-up both our Trevor and Bobby...

I had to go and see the headmaster and his deputy on my first day. The headmaster said, 'We have heard all about you young Welburn and we understand that things may be a bit strange for you until you settle in. But we do not tolerate fighting and bullying here. If we find out that you get involved you will be in here and will get six of the best! We can always send you back to that approved school, now you wouldn't like that would you?' Little did he know that's exactly what I would have liked! I didn't want to come home and join his school. It really fucked my head up that 'gap' in my life.

MALLY - THE BOY WHO FLEW THROUGH WINDOWS

It was the worst 'gap' in my entire life really. If I'd stayed at Stockton Hall for another year and fulfilled the potential that I'd been told I had at football, as a goalkeeper, at rugby, at cricket and at running, who knows where it might have taken me? I excelled at all types of sport and to come home and not be allowed to do any sporting activity whatsoever, while me Dad was at home from sea, was awful. And to go to that school and into an environment where for the very first time I saw all these lasses and everything was so different. The conduct of the kids, the rules and regulations was all different. The whole experience was very traumatic. It was a different world.

At Stockton Hall we always had to sit with our arms folded in the classroom. We had to say, yes sir, no sir. But when I arrived in this large comprehensive school where half of the pupils didn't give a shit about learning anything or improving themselves, it would have been easy to become a part of that culture and take on that mentality.

And yes, you've guessed it, later on my very first day, there was the school bully. He said he wanted to fight with me because he was 'the Daddy'. I thought, like fuck he was the Daddy. This small, skinny, little hardcase wanted to kick my fucking head in. I don't think so!

But what do you do when it's your first day at a new school?

The fight I had was with the 'cock' of the school, Rob Adams. He's now a very good friend of mine and we often laugh about our first meeting...

Well word soon got out that the fight was arranged for after school on the playing fields, behind the bushes. And by the time 3.30 came, nearly everybody knew about it and were waiting for the 'cock' of the school to kick this 'borstal' kid's head in. I don't think so.

He was known as the fastest kid in the town. In the time you blinked he'd knocked you out, or so they said. But fuck me if he was going to knock me out - I don't think so.

This so-called hardcase finally appeared. He was as thin as a lolly-stick - and he came up to me and went.

'Oy!'

It was just like a grunt, I suppose he was trying to sound hard. I said pardon, I couldn't understand him - he couldn't even talk properly. I think he was trying to say, do you want a fight? Well that wasn't a problem.

There I was in me blazer - me sports jacket - I didn't even take that off for the fight.

He had a big, big gang behind him all chanting his name.

Well there they all were.

'Rob! Rob! Rob!' they were chanting. And I couldn't believe it when I looked around and saw who was behind this kid. Guess who was chanting his name and wanting this wanker to kick ten bells of shit out of me? It was my two brothers, Trevor and Bobby!

Well bring him on!

It seemed that nearly the entire school was there as we got ready to fight. The bully and about 200 behind him - against me! I looked out of the corner of my eye and saw the headmaster and his deputy. I recalled our little meeting earlier in the day and thought, Oh fuck am I in trouble now?

But fuck it I thought - they could only send me back to Stockton Hall couldn't they?

Here's hoping! But to my surprise the headmaster gave me that nod to put this bully on his arse!

Well I'd done a bit of boxing at approved school, but fuck that, he came at me with his fist going ten to the dozen.

But every one of his punches hit me on the chest cos I just leaned back. And I got my left hand round his neck, I had a good grip, he was going nowhere. I looked across at the headmaster and he gave me the nod again.

Whether it was to say that's it, let go now, or something else, I didn't know. I maybe read him wrong.

Well there I was with this vice like grip round the 'cock' of the school. That sounds rude doesn't it but you know what I mean, the hardcase, the bully!

He wasn't going to get out of my grip. And just to make sure I gave him what I gave that evil bastard who had me scrubbing them floors, stark naked in that approved school.

I gave him a right hand. And his lights went straight out.

As he fell to the floor I screamed take that you bastard and don't fuck with me again!

I looked at all the open-gobbed kids and shouted, Does anyone else want a go? Come on I'll fight anybody!

MALLY - THE BOY WHO FLEW THROUGH WINDOWS

Come on! Who's next, yer wankers! But there was no reply. All I heard was the chant, Mally! - Mally! - Mally!

How phoney can people be?

Even our Trevor and Bobby were chanting my name.

Then our kid said, 'Run, we have to be home. I didn't think nowt of it. And then it was back to number 11...

I became a bit of a cult figure after that. The whole thing just snowballed after I'd beaten Rob Adams. It was like the old, 'the King is dead - long live the King.' To this day Rob and I have always had a laugh and a joke about it.

Funnily enough he breeds budgies now. Our Trevor used to breed budgies - I used to breed the pigeons.

It was my turn to be the 'cock' of the school where I attracted all the other kids, the 'Greenies', the twins, Terry Milner was there and we had this little gang and nobody could stop us going where we wanted to, even the sixth formers. They were the only ones who were allowed in the school at dinnertime but as soon as we turned up they let us in because they were frightened of us.

I'd have a fight nearly every day, but only when me Dad was away, I must stress. Cos when I got home I'd get beaten by me Dad if he'd found out. And after that first fight, he had found out! And when we got home, he growled,

'Where the fuck have you three been?'

Our Trevor, the grassing bastard, told me Dad I'd been fighting.

'Who with? And what for?' asked me Dad.

Oh, here we go again.

'You think you can fight do you? You black bastard, take that!' Bang!

'Now get up. Take that!'

Bang again!

Fuck me, the winner of the earlier fight was definitely the loser now! My first day at school, I'd beat the bully. Then the real bully, me Dad - beat me. I'd only been at number 11 for two days. Not much had changed then...

Then fuck me. While I was battered and sent to bed, the mother of the kid I had just beaten up came banging at our door.

Then it was, ' Get down these stairs yer black bastard.'

I'm sure me Dad must have knocked all them spots off my face that night. I didn't go to school again for about a month!

I had to wait while the swelling and the cuts healed up. Well the good Lord must have been looking down on me again because me Dad was offered the chance to go back to sea, thank fuck for that.

As I've said, we loved it when me Dad was away!

That was the time I started going out with girls and fighting all the other lads from other schools who thought they were hard. But they hadn't come across Mally Welburn had they?

They soon found out they weren't quite as hard as they thought they were when they came looking for me!

Which as I say loads did. And loads fell by the wayside.

Well you know what I said earlier on - it was stand up and fight or lie down and be beaten.

The only man that beat me was me Dad. And I always believed that no other man could ever put me on my arse. I know it's not clever and I'm not proud of the fact now. But that's just the way it was.

Do you know, I even told Sir Bobby Robson a little bit about my life when I met him. He calls me, 'The Man From The Wilderness'. I like that, 'The Man From The Wilderness'.

Anyway, where was I? Oh yes, the old man went back to sea again, at least on and off. But he never changed.

He was still the same when he came home. What with the arseholes who were too frightened to say no to him when he invited them round. No, nothing ever changed. And we still heard him beating my mother up, the bastard!

Let me tell you about the night that I planned to kill me Dad. I was fourteen at the time. It was just after he'd got home from sea. He'd beaten my Mam up again. I just couldn't take anymore. I sneaked a bread knife upstairs and hid it in Trevor's clothes. Fuck him I thought, me Dad wouldn't check our Trevor's gear.

Well anyway it was a 'party night' and we were all sent to bed early. It was only about 6 o'clock.

Much later the party came to an end without us being the entertainment. You could hear everything that was going on downstairs. At about midnight me Dad came upstairs to bed, leaving my Mam battered downstairs.

He never locked us in our bedroom that night. But we dared not move until we were certain me Dad was asleep.

It was worse than the 'bogey-man' feeling at approved school - and that's in your so-called home!

Well anyway, after about an hour Mother came up and went to bed. How she slept with him I'll never know.

I gave it another hour. It was total silence, apart from I could hear them rabbits in them sheds outside.

The sheds were full of them, all in cages. That was our job when we got home from school, to clean the rabbit cages out. And feed and water them before we could play out. It usually took the three of us - Trevor, Bobby and me - about four hours to do it all. But if you had to do it on your own it could take up to eight hours!

Then the old man would let you play out. But what was there to do at one o'clock in the morning?

I remember when the old man even rigged a load of spotlights up in the back garden so that we could dig the garden over before we could play out.

When Dad was home from sea, we always had to do the garden when we came home from school, before we were allowed to play out.

And to this day funnily enough, I hate gardening!

Anyway, knife in hand, the night I was going to kill me Dad. You could hear them rabbits banging in the shed.

Saying that it could have been the rats pinching the rabbit food or the little baby rabbits to eat. Sometimes you would see dead rabbits, the big ones, torn to bits by the rats.

But they still went in the pot for a pan of stew - mmmmm - lovely!

I also soon learnt to skin a rabbit - and catch a rat! The old man got some big rat traps. You should have seen the size of some of them rats. Saying that you just hit them with a hammer, exactly the same as the normal sized ones!

Rats! What do you do when you come across those two-legged rats that you meet in life? I'll tell yer the answer to that later. The pen is stronger than the sword?

Well there I was with my 'sword' at the age of just fourteen.

I was ready to go and kill me Dad! Trevor and Bobby were fast asleep. I crept over to Trevor's bed and got the knife. I could hear snoring. It wasn't Trevor or Bobby. I thought it must be me Dad, after all I'd never heard a lady snore before. I sneaked along the landing and opened my Mam and Dad's bedroom door. I was walking very, very slowly. It must have looked like I was sleepwalking. As I reached the side of the bed where the 'mountain' was, I remember feeling absolutely petrified. I was shaking like mad! I was too frightened to do anything. I was about to turn back but before I had the chance to change my mind it was too late.

Me Dad was that quick he sprung up from that bed and hit me like I've never been hit before in my life. You've heard the saying 'he knocked me into the middle of next week', well with me it was about three weeks! I actually woke up in hospital not even knowing how I'd got there!

I needed to get out of number 11. But I loved my Mother too much. I couldn't leave her - she was worn out, bless her!

I was glad when me Dad went back to sea again. Everybody was. I know it's not nice to wish you'd never see your Dad again, but I can honestly say I wished it time and time again.

I hadn't been home from approved school two minutes. But I'd already been battered left, right and centre.

Funny, I never saw the old man hit our Trevor or Bobby.

I once saw him hit my brother, Richard who I love. He's the closest brother I got to, I love him, our Richard. One morning my Dad gave him a really good beating and locked him in the cupboard under the stairs for the rest of the day.

What for? All he'd done was pinch a bottle of lemonade from Jack's shop on the corner of Witty Street.

Somebody was going to get the backlash for all these beatings. Don't let anyone get in my way. They wouldn't understand anyway. It wasn't them that I was fighting with. It wasn't them that I was hitting. It was me old man! I always just pictured his face and punched it as hard as I could!

The times I tried to walk away from fights. I just knew that there was not going to be another man knock ten bells of shit out of me like my old man did. So it became, get my punch in first! If they got up from that, give them twice as much. And don't stop until they went down, cos they wanted to do that to me!

I'm going to have to go into the next chapter with the rest of this story. So I'll see you in chapter seven.

Don't forget I'm only fourteen and a half at this stage of the book. I haven't run away from home yet. I haven't slept in that concrete shed on the docks yet.

Then there's the birth of my son. Then going to sea. Then detention centre and then prison. All through booze and fighting. And it didn't stop in prison, the fighting that is.

I hope you can try and understand what it was like!

See you soon, Mally.

CHAPTER SEVEN
RIDE A WHITE SWAN

That's what I wanted - to run away - but what about my Mother?

To be fair when the old man was at sea, our house was like Willy Wonker's Chocolate Factory. And if you saw our Trevor and Bobby and me, you would have thought we had found the 'Golden Ticket'. We were let loose for three weeks at least when me Dad was away. Well you can imagine can't you, look what a dog's like when you let it off the lead. And that's what we were like - mad dogs.

That reminds me we also had two big Alsation dogs, Tina and Rommy. By Rommy was really wild, he would go for anybody that came round the back of the house.

I can tell you, not many of your friends would call for you! Because there was a note on the front door that simply read, 'BACK WAY'. That's all it said. And if anybody dared venture round the back a first time - they usually never did it again! Rommy was chained up in the garden and had his own shed and compound in 'Shantyville'.

Tina was a lovely dog, Oh she was nice, she was my Dad's pride and joy - and she became mine as well. She was like a best friend to me. She would always come to me because I would always stroke her and make a fuss of her. She, like my mother was never allowed out of the house.

My mother was frightened that if she went out even to the shops, she'd to answer to my Dad about it when he got home. So I guess to avoid getting any beatings she didn't go out. The times I heard my mother cry to my Dad, 'But I only went to the shop!'

But the old man never believed her - oh how that hurt - still does when I think about it.

Anyway, when the old man was away at sea my Mam used to get something like £10 a week 'wages' sent to her on a Friday.

We were always waiting for the postman - and the breadman - and not forgetting the milkman. I soon found out all them little hiding places where people used to leave their milk and bread money.

Well, how can anybody live on £10 a week with three hungry nosed kids to feed and the rent to pay?

I used to give the money which I stole to me Mam and just leave myself with enough for a Mars bar.

But people soon realised that their money was getting used for a better purpose. When the milkman knocked at their door and asked for the four weeks money that he was owed, they soon stopped leaving the money out.

It was only pennies but you know what they say, pennies into pounds, look after the pennies and the pounds look after themselves. There wasn't a lot of money about and they said things like that even more in those days.

Trevor and Bobby dared not do owt like that of course cos they were scared in case me Dad found out!

Fuck that, I was doing it for my Mam, so she could buy herself some hairspray or a packet of cigarettes. My Mam loved her hair and she loved to smoke but she couldn't afford anything like that while me Dad was at sea.

There was also Les Demby, the man with the fruit and vegetables. He used to come round with a horse and cart. We did not pinch off Les cos he was a really nice man. Not only that, he used to give us all the old cabbage leaves and carrots. The rabbits didn't see the carrots very often, we ate them. He also gave us all his old bad apples, no wonder we had the shits half the time.

My mother always said eating a bit of bad won't do you any harm as long as you washed it before you ate it. Later on in life, I've used that saying in a few chat up lines, but not when I was only just coming up to fifteen years of age of course!

Well I soon found out where the breadman parked his van after his round. It was in the compound just over the fly-over. But there were some other lads always going there and pinching the bread and cream buns, but they were selling their's. And they were a lot older than us.

I'd got me a few mates by then, but our Trevor and Bobby tagged on at the back.

Well we met the other gang and this big pudding threatened us that if we didn't fuck off he was going to fill us all in.

You what! Here we go again!

I told him he had had his fill of cake, it was our turn now! We agreed that the winner of the fight between me and him got to raid the vans - and no coppers! Game on!

Again I didn't even take my coat off!

Bang! One punch! Goodnight!

He didn't know who I was when I hit him. But he soon found out when he woke up!

I said sorry to him when he came round a couple of hours later. He hadn't known how hungry I was!

Well anyway, we then got the chance to raid the vans. We crawled under the fence. Trevor and Bobby were on lookout. They were shitting themselves, as usual. But I'd made sure they helped. Why should I be the only one to go out and get some grub on the table? Two of my mates came into the compound with me.

Half of fat boy's mates stayed, cos we promised not to hit them if they stayed and just kept a lookout cos after all they knew the place better than we did. And in fact one of them went in with us.

There was about forty bread vans getting loaded up for the following morning. When they were filled up they were put in the compound again and a security guard would take about an hour going round checking them to see that they were all locked up securely. I think they'd got wind of the 'pudding club gang', after all they'd been hitting the compound nearly every night, so we found out afterwards...

Anyway, we were in this compound with only about fifteen vans in it and all the doors were open but there was nowt in the first few vans. You know it was them bread vans that they got the bread from the back, and at the side of the van they had like a roller shutter door that you pulled up and down where they kept all the cream buns and that. Well anyway I opened this roller shutter on one van and there was one of them wooden trays on the top shelf. I couldn't see what was in it but as I was climbing in to get the tray, my mate said,

'There's someone coming.'

I said to him to lock me in and come back for me when the

guy had fucked off. There I was in total darkness, sat in the side of this bread van. But I could get my hand up and over and could feel what was on the tray.

There was my Mother's pride - vanilla slices - a full tray of them - with six in a box. I could feel the icing on the top and when I squeezed them I could feel the custard running down my fingers.

Don't forget I was in total darkness. But in the pitch dark I felt as though I was back in Willy Wonker's again. Well, I was in a way wasn't I? I was that greedy little pig. No wonder that fat kid was how he was, I thought.

I think I ate all six from a box before my mate came back for me and lifted the shutter up and said, 'Come on Mally, we're in the wrong yard. These are the vans that are broken down, they ain't used these vans for ages!'

Well, with that I pulled the wooden tray down so that I could get the rest of the vanilla slices but to my horror the custard was all green and mouldy. They must have been there for weeks. I started to spew up - really retching - it was worse than being seasick.

I had that to come every time I went to sea and believe me there's no worse feeling than seasickness. But that's what I felt like after stuffing my face with half a dozen of those poxy vanilla slices.

Well the security guard must have heard me spewing up cos all we heard was him shouting, 'I'll get you, you little bastards,' as he ran towards us. Do you know in a funny sort of way I thought of Mr Looney...

We ran like mad, empty handed and climbed over that fence in one go. There was no way he was going to catch me, even in my condition, not for a box of poxy vanilla slices! Serves me right, I hear you say.

Unbeknown to me whilst I'd been locked in the van, fatty's mob and my mates had got loads of bread cakes and buns, enough for us all to have a good share out. But I was too sick to eat for a couple of days. My Mam said drink plenty of water and asked did you wash it before you ate it?

I had the shits for about a week after that, I was in agony, guts ache all week and the shits, and on top of all that the news that me Dad was due home, Oh fuck!

There were a couple of times that when my Dad came home he was good to us. He behaved almost like you'd expect a 'normal' Dad to behave.

He would let us go out as long as we took the dogs for a walk. Well, our house backed on to Pickering Park. We had a six-foot high fence at the bottom of our garden, over that and you were in the park.

I think that's where the rats came from, cos twenty yards from our back fence was the park lake and they had three or four big islands in the middle of the lake. There were some big white swans nesting there.

Do you know a duck we called Charlie used to come to our back fence. We used to feed it the stale bread that we got from the bread vans, it was a friendly duck.

Anyway, me Dad said we could go play out after we'd cleaned the rabbits, which didn't take a lot of cleaning when they'd just had their babies. You didn't disturb them when they had young cos if you touched the new-born rabbits, you'd find them dead the next day.

So it was clean water in them bottles that hung on the cage side, you had to get a bucket of cold water from out of the tap in the kitchen. Freezing cold in them winter months. Dip the bottle in and they all had to have fresh water twice a day.

That was a bit of a job, knocking on your own back door to ask if we can come in and get some water for the rabbits!

So we could play out as long as we took the two dogs.

Well, I went to get Tina's lead, but me Dad said,

'No, you take Rommy.'

Trevor got Tina all the time me Dad was at home. But she was mine when he was away at sea.

Rommy had never been out of the garden before! Never!

He would go for you if you went near him with a lead. But I got the choker lead, the chain lead. It was one of the rare occasions that I saw me Dad laugh was when I went to put that lead on Rommy. It was like going into the lion's den.

Rommy didn't like anybody going near him. He would go for them, and I mean go to bite them! He was vicious - he was that caged animal.

I mean you fed him through the wire of his compound. But there was I going into his den to get him. He kept going for me every time I got near him. He would show his teeth and snarl and go for me. Mad bastard! A bit like me old man, I thought.

Anyway in the end my old man told me to get out of the fucking way. He walked into that compound and the dog was like a little lamb. Even Rommy the dog was shit scared of me old man. And when me Dad said, 'Sit!' not only the dog sat down, so did me and our kid!

So there was our kid and me ready to take these two wild beasts out for a walk. Saying that Tina was usually all right - until she got with Rommy! I had Rommy, he was pulling my arm out of its socket. The last words my old man said to us as we set off was,

'Don't let them off the fucking leads.' You what?

It was that dog that had never been on a lead before in its' life. And it had never been out of that compound before either. It was dragging me down the street growling at everyone. I couldn't hold him. He was too strong! He pulled himself out of my blue fisted grip! Oh fuck! He was off!

He'd never been in the street before. Trevor ran straight home with Tina, crying. And I went running after Rommy.

Well he ran straight into the park. By the time I got to the park he was in the lake going for the swans. Oh fuck!!

The biggest swan was hissing like mad and battering the dog with its wings.

Loads of people had already gathered and were watching the unusual contest.

The dog was getting a good hiding. It was getting battered. It was drowning.

I didn't even stop to think. I just dived in and swam like mad shouting and screaming and waving the chain that he'd slipped. I was trying to fend the swan off. Then it started flapping its' wings and hissing at me at the same time. It looked massive with its huge wings opened. I was shitting myself. I thought the dog was going to die.

Somehow I got the chain round him and dragged him to the side of the lake. When I got the dog out of the water he immediately keeled over. I thought Rommy was dead. And all I kept thinking was, Oh fuck, me Dad's going to kill me as well!

I think I even started to cry. But with that, the dog came round, got up and shook itself.

Thank fuck, I thought. I made a big fuss of him and told him he was a good dog. Funnily enough he was the calmest I'd ever seen him. I think he must have been in shock. But nowt compared to the shock that was in store for me. Cos as I was taking him back home down the street, guess who was coming up the street with our Trevor? Yes, you've got it, big bad John! And did I fucking get it when I got in to number 11. He battered me all over.

Then he made me sleep with the dog in its' kennel. Saying that however, it was at least nice and warm in there with Rommy. And me and him became the best of mates.

After that, apart from the old man, I was the only one that Rommy would let into his compound. Deep down, Rommy the alsation was OK. He was just a big daft dog that needed loving. Little did me Dad know that when he kept sending me in that compound, I was going to see my other mate! He never went for me again - the dog that is! So every cloud does have a silver lining, I suppose...

We all wonder, what if? sometimes, don't we? What if?

What if only I'd run into the old man's bedroom that night with that knife and carried out my plan. You might wish I had after reading this. I often wonder what would have happened to me if I had done. How would my life have been different from that moment on? I wonder if my mother would have lived longer? I'd have been out by now, from prison that is. I'm not joking! I know one thing. If my Dad had died first, my mother would have lived the life of a Queen.

What if my Mam and Dad hadn't lost their only girl in that fire? Susan was only two at the time. What if she'd survived? Would my Dad have been a different person with his little daughter in the house? What if?

What if our Trevor had been a girl? Saying that, at times I think the old man used to treat Trevor like a girl! His nickname was 'Feather'. But I call him Rigsby because he's as tight as a duck's arse!

He's the total opposite of me. He's got fair hair. He's skinny and he always fell asleep when he had a drink. Not like me. I wanted to fight the world when I had that drink! Which for the next twenty years I did. That Lambs Rum was a killer. It did something to you. Well, it did to me, just like me Dad. As you'll find out as we go along.

Can I just say that I'm not looking for any sympathy. I don't deserve any. Just a bit of empathy will do. Fuck this 'feeling sorry for yourself' lark. There's millions dying around this world as you're reading this. As my Mother used to say, 'There's always someone worse off than you are.' And I've always believed that.

So bollocks to feeling sorry for yourself!

But let's get back to when I was coming up to fifteen years of age and not long to go before I was out into 'the wilderness'. Because when you got to school-leaving age in our house, you were out on your own. It was the same for all my other brothers, no matter what. You were out on your own, fend for yourself, on the streets in my case!

'One less to feed.' That was my Dad's motto.

'What was good enough for me when I was fifteen is good enough for you lot,' he used to say.

I can't speak for my other brothers about leaving home because as you know I never grew up with them.

I did get very close to my brother, Richard, because he used to write to me when I was in one home and he was in another. And I remember going to visit him.

We had 'inter-visits' when I was in Stockton Hall and he was in another approved school. I can't recall the name of the school but it was near Malton in North Yorkshire and it always sticks in my mind because funnily enough it was near a village called Welburn.

He showed me all these birds eggs and where the different types of birds nested. How I wished for them times all the months I was at number 11.

Richard, like me, was also a gifted footballer. He had the skill, I had the brawn. And the combination worked when I joined Richard's team in later years. Tell you about that when we get to it?

Anyway I can remember one of the last severe beatings that 'Daddy' gave me. And when I say severe beating, I mean severe beating! Here we go again...

During the early 1970s there used to be a small travelling fair that used to come to Hull and set up under Hessle Road flyover. They called it Gallagher's Fair. From Brighton Street to Gipsyville there used to be a railway line with a manual crossing. But a little later on they built a flyover over the railway lines. There was some spare land at the Gipsyville side, about an acre and that's where the travelling fair used to set up. There were waltzers, stalls and rides, a ghost train and all that. It was one of them rare occasions that we watered the rabbits, picked all the dog shit up and dug it into the garden in double quick time.

'Good for the spuds,' the old man said.

I think that's where my Mam got that saying from: 'Wash it before you eat it, cos you never know where it's been'.

Well that night when the fair was in town my Dad had just got home and the house was full again with his fishermen mates. The party was in full swing and my Mam asked me Dad if me and my brothers could go to the fair to get us out of the way. She was lovely me Mam. Got us out of the way whenever she could. Thank fuck for that. I wouldn't have to do my Elvis!

'Are the rabbits done?' the old man asked. - Yes Dad.

'Have the dog kennels been cleaned out?' - Yes Dad.

'Has the garden been dug?' - Yes Dad.

'Have the dogs been fed?' - Yes Dad.

'Have you got any money?' - No Dad!

'Well you won't be there very long then, will you?' - No Dad.

'I want you all back in this house in two hours!' - Yes Dad.

We were like three mad dogs let loose. Well I was cos Trevor and Bobby used to go to the fair every year when I'd been at approved school. But this was the first fair that I'd been to. And I wanted to go on my own.

Bobby had his friends, Trevor had his friends. I think they may have had girlfriends by then. But I never had a girlfriend cos I'd just come home from approved school. Trevor and Bobby had been brought up in the community. They knew everybody. I didn't know anyone!

It was seven o'clock when we left number 11. We arranged to meet at the top of West Grove at ten to nine. Me, Trevor and Bobby so we could all get back together by nine o'clock. Fuck going home on your own to number 11.

I got to the fair first cos I could run. Do you still remember

Mr Looney? Well I ran like that but this time it was with excitement not because of fear.

Well unbeknown to me a young lass had a ten bob note pinched off her at the fairground that night. Someone pinched it out of her hand. But what I was told was that she was telling everyone that Mally Welburn had pinched it. I didn't know nowt about it. But apparently she'd run home crying her eyes out, shouting 'Mally Welburn's pinched my money'.

Well her Dad went round banging at number 11 and told my Mam and Dad that the lass had seen me with this gang of kids running round the fair, going on all the rides.

Little did they know we were sneaking on and off the rides without paying - as you do when you don't have any money!

Well me Dad sent me Mam out looking for me.

Me Mam saw our Trevor and Bobby and told them to find me and send me home as quickly as they could.

'Tell Mally yer Dad wants him now!'

I had only been out about half an hour when our Bobby found me. And he was shaking, saying,

'You're wanted at home straight away, me Dad wants you.'

What for I said?

'I don't know but he wants you home right now!' he said.

I thought what the fuck have I done now?

I didn't know my Mam and Trevor were still looking for me. Well I ran home thinking I will still get to go back to the fair. He will only want me to do Elvis or Blakey.

'Get that bus out - Got you this time Butler!'

It was a TV show that my Dad laughed at, 'On The Buses', it was called.

Anyway as I got to the back door of number 11, I couldn't hear any party music. That's strange, I thought.

I knocked and walked in. I went through the kitchen, where Tina the dog was under the table. Then I went to the open door that led to the living room. That's where you had to stand and ask me Dad if you could please come in. Well all my Dad's mates had gone, how strange! And my mother wasn't there either. I thought she might have gone to bed or got in the bath which was upstairs.

My Dad was sitting on his settee. We weren't allowed on his settee, not when he was at home, that was. The telly was just near the door, head high where I was standing. All that was in that room was the mountain, me Dad, half pissed. Some 'Long Life' beer cans lay on the floor next to the empty chairs. And by the side of me Dad, a half drunk bottle of rum.

Did you want me Dad, I said. I was thinking, let me get back to that fair.

'Where have you been?' he asked.

I've been to the fair, Dad, I replied.

'Who with?'

Our Trevor and Bobby, Dad.

'Who else?'

Nobody Dad. I could feel myself 'frowning'.

'Frowning' was something that I did most probably out of fear, when me Dad asked me a question I didn't know the answer to. It was the look I gave when inside I was thinking, what are you talking about Dad? A puzzled look, what are you talking about? And you know the lines would appear across my forehead and me Dad would call it frowning. But I didn't even know what he meant when he shouted,

'What are you frowning for? Where have you been?'

I've been to the fair Dad.

'Have you been on the rides?'

Yes, loads Dad.

'Where did you get your money from?'

Nowhere Dad, I sneaked on the rides, Dad.

'You what?'

Then he'd ask the same questions again,

'Where have you been?'

That's when I'd end up frowning, looking puzzled and thinking, what's he on about? But I knew what was coming, I sensed it, I knew he was either going to give me a clip round the lug or give me a real beating! I sensed it!

Well he got up! The room went dark. We only had a 60 watt light bulb. But even a 100 watt wouldn't have made any difference. I thought he was reaching to turn the telly down or to switch channels. But to my surprise, he swung round and hit me. The way he clipped me on the back of my head, was in such a way that I flew into the middle of the living room. There was no escape from there. No Mother.

Oh fuck, what was all this about?

'Don't fucking lie, yer lying black bastard,' he said as he shut the kitchen door. I didn't know what the fuck he was on about. 'Where's the fucking money,' he growled.

And then, BANG!! He hit me again!

What money Dad, I asked sobbing.

'The money you pinched!'

Another full fisted punch followed - BANG!

I flew across the room again, this time hitting the wall and bouncing off it back towards me Dad.

'Get up!' he yelled. 'Where's the money?' But I couldn't reply. It felt like I'd just been hit with a sledgehammer.

BANG! I could feel my face bursting open. I wasn't worried about my spots.

'Get up!' he yelled again. 'Where's the money?'

I don't know what you're talking about, Dad.

BANG! All I could see now was them stars and silver dots - and lots of blurred colours. I didn't know where I was.

It was the worst beating that I'd ever had in my life! I was punched non-stop from wall to wall. Nobody heard my screams or my cries. Then the belt came out. I couldn't get up. He just kept yelling, 'Where's the money?'

At that stage I was 'gone'. Semi-conscious! I was unrecognisable. I looked like The Elephant Man. John Merrick had nowt on me. I was even talking like him.

With that I heard my Mam's voice. I thought I was dreaming. What little I could see out of my closed eyes was my Mother attacking my Dad. She'd jumped on his back and was hitting him and shouting, 'It wasn't him that did it. It wasn't him! They've found the ten-bob note, the girl was lying!' she screamed. And all I could hear was my Mother saying, 'You bastard, he never pinched the money! He never did it! Look what you've done to him. I'm getting the police!'

Then he hit me Mother.

I could hardly see, I couldn't speak, there was blood all over. I was on the floor curled up in a ball.

My Mam grabbed me away from that monster. I'm sorry, but that's the only word that I can think of to describe me Dad at that time. She then helped to carry me upstairs and put me to bed, I'm in tears now remembering that night!

Cos I know what he did to me Mam after that.

Next she helped me upstairs cos I was well and truly out of it. That was the worst beating I ever had...

As I lay in bed, I could hear the loud banging at the front door. It was the police! But they did nowt! It was a 'domestic'. That's what they called it in them days.

And all I could hear was my Dad screaming at the coppers, 'Come on you bastards, I'll take the lot of yer on! If you put one foot in my house I'll knock the fucking lot of you out!'

Upstairs I was sobbing. Uncontrollable tears were running down my cheeks. Blood running onto my pillow. I'm sorry to have to tell you but that's what it was like at number 11!

The coppers soon fucked off. The bastards. Even they were shit scared of me Dad.

Trevor and Bobby stayed out all that night. They dared not come home. I don't blame them, do you? But that wasn't the end of it. I was upstairs in the dark, cos he used to take the light bulbs out when we went to bed. I was motionless. It wasn't that I dared not move, it was because I couldn't. I was battered from head to foot.

Then I heard another bang on the front door. From what I could make out it was a bloke saying, 'I'm sorry Mr Welburn but it was not your lad that took the money. It was somebody else and we've got it back. Your lad had nothing to do with it.'

Well I obviously didn't see it but I later learned that me Dad flattened that bloke who tried to cross over his front door step to try and talk to him. Me Dad knocked him out with one punch. Then the coppers came back again, this time with an ambulance. But they still dared not come down the path. He let them take the bloke off the step.

What a nightmare that was! But my Mam and I were living that nightmare every day. And what do you do - even the coppers did nowt!

Then about an hour later he shouted me down the stairs.

I didn't dare go down at first, then he shouted again.

'Get down these stairs now.'

Oh no, not again I thought. My Mam came up and said, 'Come on son, he wants to see what he's done to you.'

She had taken a beating as well! It wasn't the first and I knew it wouldn't be the last.

Only a couple of weeks before, I'd come downstairs one night after being woken up by a lot of banging and arguing. My Mam was stood in the corner of the living room. She was stark naked. I'd never seen a woman totally naked before - well, only in pictures. I was shocked!

Her face was battered and bruised, her left cheek was all red and there was a trace of blood at the side of her mouth. She'd obviously just had a bit of a beating off the old man.

'Well what do you think yer black bastard? Why don't you fuck your Mother? It seems everybody else wants too!' yelled me Dad.

I just screamed, burst into tears and ran back up the stairs. What sort of a Father would do and say things like that?

My Mam helped me up out of my bed. I wouldn't let go of her. She was crying. I was crying. Every bone in my body ached but my head and face just felt numb.

When we reached the bottom of the stairs, Tina the dog had fucked off. The old man demanded my Mam go and find the dog. My Mam was a bag of nerves and didn't want to leave me alone again with the Monster, me Dad. But luckily when she opened the front door, there was Tina, cowering and shaking on the doorstep. She came up to me. Then me Dad said, 'Kitchen!'

I was about to go to the kitchen when he said,

'Not you, the dog, you sit down.'

That was a struggle. Then he gave me a half pint glass which he filled with Lambs Navy Rum. That was his answer to everything.

'Now get that down yer,' he said. 'And here's half a crown.'

I tried to sip the rum but there was blood dripping into the glass from my mouth. Both my front teeth were broken and my top and bottom lips were as big as Mick Jagger's.

My eyes were nearly shut.

I sipped the rum very slowly. It was horrible.

'Get it down you,' he said again. 'Then get back to bed and you can stay off school tomorrow.'

He'd beaten me so severely that the veins on the side of my head were sticking out. I was six-foot tall and built like that well known shithouse door, but I never stood a chance against me Dad. I had to stand there while he punched me in the face. You couldn't retaliate against yer Dad. My nose was broken.

My lips were all split. And I was off school for five or six weeks. But after that I never feared any other man.

Not after witnessing him beating me Mam up with them punches, with them stamps of the feet, and me Mother in the corner, cowering, crying, screaming, and I had to stand there and watch it all - the fucking evil bastard!

Then get yourself to bed. Then he'd creep up the stairs. Well he thought he was creeping up the stairs. He thought we couldn't hear him but with the size of the guy the stairs always creaked and we knew he was there.

Dad was coming! We weren't allowed to move, we weren't allowed to talk, we weren't even allowed to cough! Then we'd hear the bolt on our door and we knew we were locked in for the night. And at least we knew when he was going down the stairs as well - there was always that same creak.

But never to this day has he once said he was sorry for what he did. Not once! There was one occasion when I'd just lost me Mother. She died on Sept 18 1990 - she was only sixty-two. When I arrived home for the funeral, I got my Dad on his own, he was crying his eyes out. I said to him, Dad you was an evil bastard. Why? Why did you do it all? Why were you like that with your own family? All he said was,

'I don't know.'

There must have been some reason for it Dad? I said. Why? But he couldn't answer. All he said was that we were all bastards! 'You were all bad!' he repeated over and over again. But why did you have to do that to us? Why did you have to beat ten bells of shit out of us all the time? And why did you beat me Mother up?

'I don't know,' he repeated. That's all he ever said. The last time I saw him was about three or four years ago at my Uncle Ted's funeral but I didn't speak to him. The last time I actually spoke to him was when I rung him up the Christmas before last to try and make my peace with him. I know he's knocking on a bit now but I said now then Dad its me Mally. And he said, 'Who?'

I went, Mally

He said, 'Mary?' I went, no Mally.

And he said, 'I don't know ya, sorry.'

I went, It's fucking Mally, Trevor's twin.

'Mally? Trevor's twin?' he said. 'Sorry, have you got the right number?'

I went, Fucking hell Dad, it's me, who you used to call 'the fucking black bastard.'

'Oh Mally,' he said at last, 'How are ya son?'

I'm all right, I said. I want to come down and see ya.

'Yeah,' he said. Come down any time son. I keep hearing you on the radio and all like that.' Yeah, well I want to come and make me peace with you, I said.

'My doors open any time son,' he said. 'Is it you Mally? Is it really you?' But I just haven't been down - I just never went... My daughter tried going down but he doesn't know her and he wouldn't recognise her. And he's one of them now who wouldn't open the door - he'd just look through the window. My daughters are 25 and 21. He's taken a shine to my brother's son and his wife, who do a lot of running about for him. He's now a frail old man and they've taken pity on him, but those memories will stick with me and my other brothers. What we witnessed, what he did to me Mam, they'll stay with us forever. Some of the things he did are unforgivable...

After that beating, he was home for six weeks cos his ship was getting what they called surveyed, ship repairs. Six weeks in that house! I never went outside for them six weeks. But saying that he never hit me once during them six weeks and he never had any parties either. Maybe it was because he had to go to work on his ship every day. He was a chief engineer.

He never hit me Mam either. She had to write a note to school to say that 'I was off to help me Mam, cos she was poorly'. Bobby and Trevor were told not to say owt at school.

Mind you it was great that six weeks cos when big, bad John went to work and Trevor and Bobby were at school me Mam and me got the playing cards out. Those were the days, my friend. Me and the pal of my cradle days.

My Mother. Oh how I miss her...

That's it for now.

Some painful memories there - but hey - that was then.

Hope you are OK. I can't wait for chapter eight.

How could I leave my Mother? See you in eight.

Take care now - Mally.

CHAPTER EIGHT
STAYIN' ALIVE

'Stayin' Alive' was another favourite record of mine by The Bee Gees. And whenever I think of the Bee Gees I think of me hands and knees, which we had to get on to scrub the dog kennels out. And them rabbit cages, the ones that were on the bottom row, they were about three foot wide and two foot deep and about eighteen inches high, that's where the rats used to run across the shed floor.

Every night when we came home we had to do the garden. And we were supposed to take it in turns to go to the shop.

But it was usually me who went. Trevor and Bobby were at home - Richard had flown the nest - so it was usually me.

The garden looked like a shantytown, all the sheds with all the rabbits in. It was a shantytown.

It was all made out of interior doors which me old man had got when they'd been demolishing Brighton Street.

They were very solid sheds with tin sheets for the roofs.

They stretched the full length of one side of the garden - and we had one of the biggest and widest gardens in Gipsyville.

It was about 150 foot long by about 70 foot wide. It was split by a little two-foot path leading right to the bottom.

On the right as you walked down was the 'rabbit factory'. We could have any pets we liked with my Dad as long as we looked after them. Richard got the pigeons first and I got them later on. But it was the rabbits that took over! My Dad used to breed them, kill 'em and sell 'em every Christmas - if the rats hadn't got them that is. He didn't make anything out of it, they weren't worth a light really. But I don't think he could see it - the old man loved them. He loved his big New Zealand whites. He had all different kinds and they certainly did breed like rabbits.

Later on, our Trevor was the budgie man, he liked his budgies, I was the pigeon fancier.

MALLY - THE BOY WHO FLEW THROUGH WINDOWS

I used to race pigeons but unfortunately had to stop cos I kept falling off the roof. Boom! Boom!

And I used to have greyhounds as well. I had four winners in one night once. But I had to get rid of them because one of them bit the ex-wife. She had a harelip! Boom, boom!

But I'll tell you more about them later on...

On the left of the path the garden was split into three. The first bit was for the bed of roses which me Mam loved. Then there was Rommy's compound, for that 'beast' of a dog, a plot of about twenty foot square including compound and kennel, with a big wire mesh fence around it. He needed that fence. He always went crackers when Tina was on heat. That's why we had to keep Tina in the house, but I could handle Rommy by then.

The rest of the garden was all soil, which is what we had to keep weed free. We were in for it if me Dad saw a single weed. You would have thought it was well kept the amount of time we spent on it. I suppose it was in a strange sort of way. He, me Dad, planted spuds and cabbages and right at the bottom of the garden we had an apple tree. The apples always gave us bellyache. They were crab apples, I think that's what they call them. We used to throw them at the kids in the park instead of bricks. We used to love it when someone would set up with their fishing rod, cos as I say our back fence backed onto the park and it had a big lake. Lots of people used to go fishing there.

Well anyway we would wait till the fisherman got set up with his rod and nets and everything. And while he was watching his float we would be out of sight. Behind our shed was the perfect hiding place. And apples at the ready.

We would whistle knowing that the bloke would look round. At the exact second he looked round to see who was whistling, the apple was on its way into the lake. It was precision stuff! The number of times you heard them fishermen say they hadn't had a bite all day but there had been plenty of rises, fish coming to the top. It took them a while to realise that it was us. Maybe it was cos the apples floated. I think that might have given them a bit of a clue! But when we got a bit tired of that little game, I came up with a better idea. That was rather than throwing the apples into the lake, we'd throw them at the blokes who were fishing instead. By, I was a really good shot! Time and time again I hit my targets. It wasn't long before one of the harder blokes came over to our fence screaming at us, 'Get over here yer bastards, I'll kick yer fucking heads in. Get yer arse over here!'

You what, I would shout back.

'Over here', they would say.

I didn't need a second invite, I was over that fence and BANG! Take that yer bastard! I would say as I was punching his lights out. I must stress we only did that sort of thing when the old man was away - and during the apple season!

It was my grounding. I was beating-up grown men at the tender age of fifteen. I'm painting a picture for you, and I know it looks bad doesn't it?

I never ever smacked our Trevor or Bobby because they knew not to fuck with me. And I lost count of the number of fights I got into cause somebody picked on my twin and younger brother. Back then I looked after them. But recently, at the age of forty-six, our Trevor acceded the dizzy heights of Black Belt, fifth dan in karate, ah! you what?

I never got into all that stuff where you weren't allowed to hit anyone. I believed punch first - ask questions last!

I used to watch them train on the park. Jack Cochran, bless him. The Cochrans were a great family and Jack, their Dad, he was the Karate man! The hardest man on Gypsyville, they said. Well, if he was that hard why didn't he come and sort the old man out? The times I wished he had.

I remember him years later when I was fishing. I had a house-warming party with all my trawler mates and Jack was there. He ended up in intensive care after getting a bottle of Lambs Navy Rum over his head, all over a bet.

I got six months in detention centre for that. That was my first spell behind bars. But I'll tell you more about that later...

Do you know I've always wondered why do people call me 'Mad Mally'?

I think we will find out by the time we get to the end of this book. I'm still only fifteen at this stage. I'd got over that beating off me Dad. But I still bear the scars of it to this day, mentally.

I didn't have long to go at Kingston High School. What time I spent there that is. But I got into the school football team as a striker cos they already had a very good goalkeeper. And believe me they even let me train in bare feet. Who the fuck was Zola Budd? She wasn't even on the scene then - so she must have literally followed in my footsteps!

Who was Mike Tyson? He made millions fighting, not boxing. I tried that boxing lark. What? Wearing gloves? It wasn't for me. All I wanted to do was go out there and just bang them! But no, you were not allowed to do that. You had to lead with yer left, jab, jab, one two, one two. Not for me, I just wanted to knock the fuckers out. I just pictured me old man in front of me!

I loved street fighting. The bigger the bloke, the better. You know, the bigger they come, the harder they fall.

That was to become my way of life when I left number 11. Which wasn't far off, only about six months away.

Standing on my own two feet. You what! I couldn't wait...

Well the old man's ship broke down and he was due to be at home for about eight weeks - Oh! Nightmare on Shantyville! Here we go again, happy as can be. Like fuck! Happy days my arse. I used to watch the Fonz in Happy Days much later on. Happy Days? There were no happy days for me when me old man was home.

Another crazy thing he made us do was to make sure we got home from school as quick as possible. Me Dad once asked me, 'What time does the school bell go?'

I said, about half past three Dad.

'What time does the school bell go?' he asked again.

Half past three, Dad, I replied again.

He asked yet again, 'What time does the fucking school bell go? Now then.' I thought what's he talking about, I again replied half past three.

'I want to know exactly what time the school bell goes,' he said. And I had to go to the headmaster and ask him.

I said, Sir, My Dad wants to know what time does the school bell go at the end of afternoon lessons?

'When I decide to ring it,' the headmaster replied.

But he wants to know exactly what time it goes Sir.

'When I decide to ring it,' he repeated.

'It might go at twenty-nine minutes past. It might go at thirty-one minutes past. What do you want to know for Welburn?' It's my Dad who wants to know Sir.

'Well tell your Dad if he wants to know, tell him to come here and ask me.'

Oh you don't want him to do that Sir, I said.

I thought I'd better go to the 'better' side. It goes at thirty-one minutes past I told me Dad.

'Well I want you home at thirty-two minutes past three then. I want you home in a minute,' he insisted.

Now from Kingston High School to our house I would say was about half a mile. And there was no way we could hope to get home by 3.32!

So I always hoped that the bell would go at 3.29 to give us three minutes to get home.

And we had to run as fast as we could to get home, get round the back of the house, knock on the back door and wait for him to say, 'Come in!'

Then we could go in and he'd say, 'What took yer?'

And he'd be watching the clock.

They were a bit late ringing the bell today, Dad, we'd say.

But if we were a minute or two late, he'd give us that clip around the ear and say, 'Don't fucking lie.'

It was quicker to cut through the park and jump over the fence, it was only six feet high but he'd never let us jump over the fence.

We had to go round. When the bells toll!

The only good thing I can remember me Dad doing was when he was going to be home for more than them three days, he would fill the pantry up with tinned food. And I'll give him his due, he didn't buy the cheap shit what we sometimes had to eat when the pantry was empty and he was away at sea.

He used to make a shopping list out for us. I can still remember it like it was yesterday.

6 tins of beans (Heinz)

6 tins of spaghetti (Heinz)

6 tins of tomatoes (Plum)

6 tins of Fray Bentos pies - by, they were nice, what we got of them that is. I used to pick the hard crust that stuck to the rim after it was cooked in the oven for about forty minutes and

after the old man had a full one to himself. But it was nice to pick at the empty tin, before it went in the dustbin. They still do them pies today, sell them that is.

I must stress no food ever went in the dustbin, it was just the empty tins. If we didn't eat what little was left over, the dogs got it. If the dogs didn't get it, the rabbits did. And if the rabbits didn't get it, the rats did!

6 small bags of tatties

Tatties always reminded me of that bonfire and Mr Looney. For all I know me Dad and Mr Looney could have been brothers. Just think about it. Mr Looney wanted to kill me. What was me Dad trying to do to me?

6 half a dozen boxes of eggs

Try saying that six times quickly, it's OK for you I've got to write it or type it. And I'm doing all this with one finger - not bad is it? Nowt wrote down, no notes to work from, it just all comes flowing back.

Oh, we had to open the boxes of eggs before we got them to make sure none were broken. And God help us if we fetched one home cracked, never mind broken. We would get a crack from me dad and have to take them back to the shop.

The number of times we had to take some back and the shop wouldn't accept them.

'They were all right when you took them,' the woman in the shop would say. Fuck that, we just had to pinch another box when nobody was watching. That was better than getting that smack off me Dad. And take home the one or two eggs that had been cracked and on the way home crack the other four eggs and eat them raw, they were nice raw eggs. I used to drink about eight raw eggs with a bit of milk when I was at sea. Because we could eat what we liked at sea. Well you worked hard for your grub!

I can't wait to tell you about my fishing days. Some really hard bastards used to go to sea. I believed all the hard bastards went to sea. You had to be hard to go to sea, I always thought. And I'll tell you what, we should get some of these so-called hardcases of today and bang them aboard a sidewinder trawler. We should send them deep water fishing with the most evil bastard of a skipper. Send them to sea for up to twenty-four days working 18 hours on and 6 off in storm force weather. Getting knocked from port to starboard. We'd soon see how tough these so-called hardcases are!

Hey, getting knocked from port to starboard didn't bother me a bit, it was better than getting knocked from wall to wall by me Dad!

I got to love it at sea. I was grafting and getting three or four good meals every day. I would love to see today's hardcases do just one trip aboard a sidewinder trawler, like The Arctic Corsair. You can go and visit The Arctic Corsair cos it's now a floating museum. It's berthed on the River Hull behind the Transport Museum down High Street in Hull City centre.

I recommend you go and have a look round if you get the chance. It's a real eye-opener just to see the size of the trawler. It's tiny. Imagine what the conditions aboard must have been like! The last ever sidewinder trawler that sailed out of Hull. While you're there ask to see the ship's log book. You'll see my name and the other lads I've mentioned. Ask that old sea-dog, that old fisherman who will give you that guided tour, unpaid, they do it for the love of it, to show you the log. It's what we signed when we signed on the ship but don't forget to give the old sea-dog a back-hander, money I mean, because the fishing industry was built on back-handers. I'll tell you more about them later as well...

But before we go back to getting all them rations as we used to call them, shopping, you know - filling the pantry - when me Dad was home, I must just tell you a bit about my very first trip on the Arctic Corsair.

The Arctic Corsair was owned by the Boyd Line. I had just come out of prison and my old company Hamlyns had scrapped most of their trawlers. All their trawlers were named after Saints. Some of the ones I sailed on were:

The St Dominic - that was my very first trip to sea. I was 16 at the time.

The St Jason - that was the best ship I ever sailed on. The skipper was Arthur Ball and it had a great set of herbs, that's what we called the crew, Brian Risdale was the mate.

The St Jerome - the Platens - all the family seemed to be on there, Gary - a herb, Ray, Gary's brother in the galley, and their dad Terry.

The St Benedict - Doyley and his Diddymen, Trevor the

skipper and his favourite herbs known by everybody as his Diddymen. Caddy, Jeff, Smithy and Egor, he'd go anywhere for his skipper, Albo and the others.

The St Jasper - I sorted a few bullies out on that ship.

The St Lorman - And I earned some money on that one! I sailed on all of those ships and I'll tell you all about them as we go along. Funny, I was born on St Georges Day. And I lived in a 'cave' down St James Street. You never know, they might make me a Saint one day for bounce-back-ability.

Well anyway my trip aboard the Arctic Corsair.

I had been on a big walkabout - out of work, to you. Boyd Line was looking for a crew for the Arctic Corsair and they couldn't find a third hand officer.

You had to have a bosun's ticket, which I had - and you had to go to fishing school to achieve your qualifications, which I did. I got 99.9% on a mock radar observer's course. So I could navigate a ship. Clever I hear you say! I used to love it being on the bridge of a ship, especially when it was my watch and I had to navigate. By, the times we saw them shooting stars.

I was at Hamlyns for a long time. A lot of fishermen used to chop and change from one company to another but I stayed with Hamlyns all the time until I did my first spell in prison. When I came home from prison they'd decommissioned about half the trawlers. Hamlyns was one of the companies that suffered. They didn't have any trawlers left - they went bust, belly up. I was thirty years old in 1988 - you can still see my name in the log-book.

Well I signed on the Arctic Corsair. It was her first trip back to sea after being laid up for years. She was a 'rust bucket' but any work was better than none at all, so I signed on as third hand. This is a good little yarn...

Anyway the only other problem with the Arctic Corsair at the time, was the skipper. He had a bad reputation. Some said that he was a real evil bastard and he didn't give a fuck about his crew. I soon found out that both those facts were not far from the truth! They were looking for a crew but because of the skipper's reputation, few people would sail with him. But I wanted the work desperately and said I'll sail with him. To protect the innocent, we'll call him Sir Bernard. At sea you always called the skipper, 'skipper'. It showed respect. They'd earned it, well, some of them had. And you didn't sit in his chair on the bridge - a bit like being at number 11! But there couldn't be anybody worse than me old man, could there?

I didn't know any of the crew apart from the bosun, Dave Lilley. Dave is a great guy in more ways than one. He's helped me loads of times. He was one big guy back then, about twenty-five stones of him. He was like a barrel.

Do you know nowt ever got Dave down. No matter what happened to him, he always laughed things off! I guess everyone has a breaking point though and I witnessed Dave's. But even then, in the end, all that we could do was laugh!

Well we set sail and with the ship being laid up for that length of time hardly anything aboard worked properly. We spent every working hour, 18 sometimes, getting all the fishing gear ready. You know, the nets, the bobbins, the trawl, the doors etc. etc. We did it while we were steaming to the fishing grounds. Bear Island we were heading for, not far from Russia. If you look at a World map, England and Bear Island are only about two inches apart. But don't be fooled, it was a long, long journey!

We used to navigate by charts, our plotter - red, purple and green - and radar. A plotter is a navigational aid. Any seaman will know it. On your chart you have three lines, one green, one red and one purple and when you take a bearing where the lines cross, that's where you are on the chart.

Today of course there's all modern technology with satellite navigation and everything, the ship can steer itself now.

Well anyway the officers had to take a watch to navigate us safely to the fishing grounds. We would work six hours on the bridge, six hours in yer bunk, 12 hours on the deck. I always followed Dave on watch. He used to spend an hour teaching me how to read the stars. I read mine in the paper now - I'm the bull!

And some of the stories Dave told me really made me laugh. By he was a funny man. But saying that, I met a lot of funny fishermen. Some of them were happy to make you laugh while you did the graft. I didn't mind that though.

We finally got to the fishing grounds. Everything was ready. The weather was about a force 6, a bit rough! We were rolling from side to side. We could hear the plates smashing in the galley, falling out of the plate racks. Then the skipper gave the magic words 'down trawl'. That meant lower the nets into the water. We all had our brand-new 'duck suits', waterproofs on, which cost about £40 for top and bottoms. That was a lot of money in the 1980s! You only took one pair with yer to last yer the whole trip. Some took two pairs, they must have been the non-drinkers. Gear not beer was their saying. Well fuck buying a new duck suit every trip. Then it was all hands on deck to get the net in the water. That was it, 18 and 6. That was 18 hours of work and 6 hours sleep - fishing hours. The mate and the skipper would be on the bridge sharing the fishing hours. Remember I followed Dave on watch. The nets were in the water. You usually towed yer trawl for four hours. This was the first time that the fishing gear had been used, the first time it had been in the water for about three years.

Well the nets hadn't been in the water an hour, and the old man, the skipper sang out, 'Hauling time'. That meant it was time to get the nets in - a storm force ten was coming our way! 'Get the gear in quick and batten down the hatches,' he yelled. Well the winch wouldn't work. Sommat was wrong down in the engine room. The ship's lights kept going out. It was total darkness. Then the ship lost all power. We were tossed all over. The waves were turning into mountains and crashing down on us. All hands were on deck waiting for the winch to start. We had about half a mile of cable to get in and then the trawl. The winch would start, run for a few seconds but then cut out. And it couldn't take it. The waves were really crashing down on us. We had somebody forward of the ship and when one of these huge waves came rolling up he would shout, 'Sea!'

The warning was relayed down the deck in just enough time to give everyone enough time to grab on to anything, which was fixed firmly to the ship. Cos when that wave hit you it would sweep you and everything else in its path overboard.

I lost count of the number of times when the full deck was under the sea...

Well all the young, fit blokes clung on for their lives. But poor old Dave just stood there and took the full weight of one of the waves. Well he was simply swept off his feet and just went floating by us like that big whale, banging his head along the way. Well he was just floating up and down the deck.

The wave swept him to the arse end of the ship where the entrance to the crew's accommodation was and he managed to scramble to safety. We didn't notice him missing you had to look after yerself. Fuck this 'one hand for yourself and one for the ship' lark! There was no way you was going to get to launch one of them life rafts. Time and time again the waves crashed down on us. Time and time again the ship's power cut out. And you still had to get yer nets in. Then one of the cables parted! Fuck me! We're never going to get the gear in, I thought. A 'one-ended job' it was called - and that's one of the worst jobs you could get when you were fishing.

There are two cables that come from your winch and if one of those parts, it's self explanatory, it's known as 'a one ended job'. And if you've only got one cable fetching in what two cables should be fetching in, all the strain is on that one single cable. We refer to the broken cable as warp. And all of it can be wrapped around the net and the doors. You've got to get all that in by hand. And in storm force weather, it could take anything up to 36 hours to get just that one job done.

And that was the first time we'd put the gear in the water!

All that was on the very first day of fishing! Twenty to go! And a storm-force ten coming our way - for fuck's sake!

Well the winch all of a sudden got to full power but we were only pulling one cable in. The ship gained full power, thank fuck, but the seas were still crashing down on us! The skipper managed to get the ship's bow to the wind and the ship was riding the waves. You could still see the seas coming though and when it came crashing down on you, you just had to cling on for dear life.

About an hour passed and Dave managed to get back on the deck. He'd changed his clothes and put on his second brand new duck suit. He was such a big man, his must have cost about £60 each! One second he was alongside of me but then another mountain of a wave came and swept him away again. There he was again, the whale, floating up and down the deck! And same again, another bang on the head, he must have been battered and bruised. He was swept down to the accommodation entrance again. And he was gone for another couple of hours.

Well we were getting to the stage where we could see the trawl doors, about a ton in weight each. And they had crossed over each other. That was worse than 'a one ended job'. A good 12-hour job to put right - on a good day!

Then another 18 hours, getting another set of gear ready. We were in for a long couple of days and we hadn't got the gear in yet and it was still only our first fishing day at sea!

What a nightmare!

What the fuck did I join that outfit for? I asked myself!

Everyone was drenched, soaked to the bone, freezing cold, you couldn't feel yer hands!

Well we got the first door in board. But all the cable was wrapped round the trawl door.

Don't ask how we got the nets in but somehow we managed it. But they were all ripped, a new trawl net was needed!

But we still had to get the other door in. Then Dave made another guest appearance. And guess what? He had another brand new duck suit on.

He came and got stuck into making the gear that we'd got inboard safe, by chaining it down. He was very clever sorting a mess like that out! But the sea takes no prisoners. And guess what? Another monster of the sea came rolling up. We could all see it coming. Everyone shouted, 'Sea!!!!'

We all clung to the ship's rigging and what ever else we could cling to, but not Dave!

He just stood there and screamed, 'Come on then, take me if you can.' Well the monster wave did just that. And back he went again to the accommodation entrance!

But this time he wasn't gone long. Only about twenty minutes in fact. And when he came back he was wearing nothing except his 'birthday suit'. Not a stitch of clothing on! Absolutely stark, bollock naked! Nowt on! Oh, what a bonny sight he was.

Well we couldn't do anything but burst out laughing. I've never seen a twenty-five stone man in the nude. That vision will stick with me till the day I die.

Well the skipper was screaming orders out of the bridge windows. But Dave said, 'Fuck this.'

He climbed up the ladders to the bridge veranda. You weren't ever allowed up there. But he went and it took him a good twenty minutes, what with those seas still crashing down on us. I've never seen a twenty-five stone bloke's arsehole before but you couldn't do nowt but look at it! When he got to the top, Dave apparently asked the skipper,

'Is your mother a fucking German, Sir Bernard?'

That was it! And I think that was also the end for Dave. He never came back after that trip! Being swept up and down the deck three or four times was his breaking point. And he cracked when he came out in the buff and climbed up onto the bridge.

All the gear was fouled. We couldn't get our head to wind. And we couldn't get a lee-side. The seas were coming down on us, Dave couldn't hold onto anything so he just let the force of the sea swill him down the deck. He was a big man. He was like that beached whale being swept along three or four times. Then the last time he appeared it was with no clothes on.

I saw the ring of fire! It was the 'end' of Big Dave!

We were twenty-eight days, dock to dock. And it took us twenty-four hours to get that gear in and another thirty-six hours to repair it all. It was all done in storm force weather and you know what? when we got home we landed in debt.

We never picked up a penny!

We'd been at sea for twenty-eight days, working 18 hours a day. But when we got home the fish we landed was rotten! That very first day in that storm had fucked up the cooling system!

That was just one slice of life aboard the Arctic Corsair. She faced a lot of problems when she went back to sea after being laid up for such a long time. But the storm force weather didn't crack us.

That wasn't true about Dave though. He never came back for another ride on the life of the ocean waves.

I made another two trips on the Arctic Corsair after that, until I had my run-in with Sir Bernard. I'll tell you more about that later. Sorry about jumping into that story but I just had to...

Before we were side-tracked, I recall we were going shopping for them six tins of beans and that.

I'll tell you what happened when we did in the next chapter.

I'll also tell you why I left home all because of a bottle of red Daddies Sauce - they never had Heinz Tomato Sauce.

And I got it over my head when I got in the house with it.
Allow me to tell you about that in chapter nine.
Take care now, Mally.

CHAPTER NINE
PUT YOURSELF IN MY PLACE

Well there we were, Trevor, Bobby and me, with the shopping list which was as long as some of these chapters.

You've got the picture, well you will as we go along.

6 tins of beans, 6 tins of spaghetti, etc. etc.

Trevor was the one who held the money. And the one thing me Dad insisted on which he would always shout at us when we were going out the back door was, 'Don't forget the fucking receipts! And don't come back until you've got everything on that list. And only get what it says on that list!'

Oh fuck, it was one big challenge.

Well to get everything on that list we had to go in about five different shops. Bread - large uncut loaf and make sure it's fresh - from Skelton's. Me Dad used to get two of them uncut loaves all for himself. He would get two sandwiches out of one loaf what with half a pound of ham in each sarnie.

2 large custard pies - we were in the shit if they only had one. And he wouldn't accept two small ones instead because they worked out dearer. We were lucky to see any custard pies - but I saw them that day, all right.

Next door to Skeltons was Ron Sewell's fruit shop.

2 pounds of bananas - and we dared not eat a banana on the way home cos the old man would know. They couldn't be single bananas, they had to be full bunches and Ron knew that.

2 pounds of cooking onions, 2 turnips, 4 pounds of big carrots, 2 cauliflowers, 6 oranges and 6 pears...

A big bunch of grapes - and we had to make sure none had been plucked from the bunch - Ron knew that as well.

2 melons if he had them - they were a treat for us sometimes. My mother used to say it was the only time we got our ears washed was when we ate a slice of melon. It still makes me laugh when I'm eating one nowadays.

2 pounds of eating apples - not them fucking crab apples the old man used to say. Anyway Ron knew me Dad was home so he always gave us the best and a little bit extra. He knew where we were coming from. When he saw me and our Trevor and Bobby walk in the shop he used to say,

'Hey up, their Dad's home, they won't pinch nowt today.'

Les Demby got his fruit and vegetables from Ron and sometimes he would be in Ron's shop and he would say, 'I better get round there and drop them cabbage leaves and old carrots off,' because me Dad used to give him a back-hander. I don't think me Dad knew my mother had a 'slate' with Les.

Funnily enough I was in Ron's the other day and he said, 'I used to love it when your Dad came home at Christmas Mally, cos he used to come in and spend £20 on fruit. And twenty quid was a lot of money then.'

And I'll give the old man his due that when he came home he filled the cupboards up, even if most of it was for himself.

Cos he could trench, he could really eat!

And in Ron's the other day he said, 'I can remember it like it was yesterday, Mally. Your Dad would always say,

'Make sure there's no grapes missing off the bunch.'

To this day the old man still gets his bananas from there.

Anyway me and Trevor and Bobby used to leave Ron's with a box of fruit and vegetables each and about two carrier bags full of grapes and the soft fruits like strawberries and that.

Oh and about ten pounds of spuds, the big ones, so we could make big, fat chips.

Then we had the stuff from Skeltons, the bread and cakes and that. Then it was off to the chemist's. Only one of us used to go in there. The other two would stand outside and keep an eye on the shopping. Saying that nobody dare touch our stuff, you what! I would have kicked their fucking heads in. I didn't want my fucking head kicked in by me old man, did I?

Look what happened when I got accused of stealing that ten-bob note off that young lass at that fair, the lying little bastard. So can you imagine what would have happened if we'd lost me Dad's twenty-pound note, or any of his change that was left? Checking your change when you came out of every shop as you went along was a must. And checking the money against the receipts and writing down on the receipts what shop that receipt came from. Cos we had to check each and every item in front of me Dad when we got home.

So you had to make sure what was on that list. We would have a pencil with us and tick things off as we went along. So the fruit shop was all present and correct. As was Skeltons, apart from instead of two large custard pies we had to get him one large and two small ones. Well it saved going home with only one didn't it? Like fuck it did that day! By the way, I'll warn you now, this is the day I left number 11!

I didn't know that when I was stood waiting outside of the Chemist with our Bobby of course. Waiting for our Trevor to get the box of Radox bath salts and some Steradent tablets.

They were to soak the old man's and mother's false teeth in. My mother used to take her false teeth out and chase you round the living room with them in her hand, pulling faces and farting and saying, 'More tea Vicar?' By, she was funny me mother, we had some great laughs together. But she never did anything like that in front of the old man. Never!

Anyway, I'd got our Trevor's box of fruit and vegetables on top of mine, leant up against the chemist window, under his canopy, because by now it was pissing down with rain.

It's all flowing back to me now, what happened I mean, not the rain, cos as I say this was the day! One giant step for mankind. If we hadn't had a roof on our house I think I could have been the first boy in space!

The Chemist was saying to our kid, 'Tell your brother not to lean on my window - and get out from underneath the canopy.' Our Trevor came out to tell us that he wouldn't serve him unless we stopped leaning on his window and moved off his front. Well those two boxes were getting heavy and I couldn't put them on the floor because the boxes were made of cardboard - and cardboard and water don't mix - and as I say it was pissing down with rain. Well I got to the shop door. I couldn't get through his door with two boxes so I just shouted out to the guy. For fuck sake mate we only want a box of poxy Radox and some Steradent tablets.

'Who are you swearing at?' he said.

I said, Who do you fucking think? Silly bastard!

Well he came running round his counter and started to man handle me out of his shop doorway and into the pouring rain.

MALLY - THE BOY WHO FLEW THROUGH WINDOWS

What! And I had these two big boxes in my arms, which were getting heavy and my hands were tied so to speak. He said, 'Go get yer Radox from somewhere else, I don't want you in my shop.' I said I ain't been in your robbing, bastard shop!
Then he looked me in the eye and said,
'Well fuck off then or I'll get the police.'
Our Trevor said to me, 'I'm telling me Dad of you'.
What the fuck had I done? Get one of these boxes I said to our Trevor. My arms had gone numb! You tell me Dad and I'll kill yer, I said.
He said, 'Well what we going to do? Me Dad will kill us both if we don't get his Radox.'
Radox was the only bath salts me Dad would use. We weren't allowed a bath in it, soap and water is what we had to use. Saying that me Mam used to leave the bath in and I'm sure she used to pinch some of my Dad's Radox. Cos I remember me Mam saying go jump in the bath. It was nice! I said to Trevor, Jacksons sell it and it's cheaper.
Our kid said me Dad said we had to get his Radox from the Chemist cos it was better from the Chemist.
What are you talking about I said, it's the same fucking stuff! He won't know the fucking difference. For fucks sake let's hurry up, these boxes are fucking heavy.
The old man had never been shopping on Gipsyville. So what difference would it make if we could get the self and same product from a different shop on our way back home - and cheaper as well. It made a lot of difference! We saved money! But no, we had to get that poxy Radox from the Chemist. Well we couldn't cos the bloke in the Chemist wouldn't serve us and our Trevor would tell me Dad and I would get the blame again. All because I was leaning on the window with two big boxes in my arms afraid to put them on the floor cos you know what it's like if you get a split bag of groceries, the contents fall out the bottom.
Well the cardboard boxes were getting wet and we still had three more shops to go in yet. For fuck sake lets hurry up cos the boxes were getting wet and heavy, I said.
Next was Frank Dees. It was a small supermarket. There we got his 6 tins of Fray Bentos steak and kidney pies - mmmm I could just eat one now. Trevor was in and out of Frank Dees

with me carrying the two boxes, walking on to the next shop, Jacksons. That was the shop that we had to get the 6 tins of everything from, you know the beans, tomatoes etc.

Then the cornflakes, butter, four bottles of milk, lard for the chips, dog food - it had to be the big tins of Chappie dog food. Well I think you've got the picture, more boxes and carrier bags. The last thing you bought was the eggs, you didn't want them falling out the box did you? So we always put the eggs gently on top of the bread and the other soft things.

Well me Dad would have nothing else but Heinz tomato sauce. It had to be Heinz!

'Don't dare fetch any ketchup in number 11, unless it's Heinz tomato ketchup.'

Well Jacksons never had any Heinz tomato sauce. There was a new brand sauce that had just come on sale. It was called Daddies Sauce, yes how apt I thought, Daddies Sauce.

Show your Dad that you love him, and buy Daddies Sauce, suggested the adverts. For your loving Dad. He'll love Daddies Sauce. Show your Dad you care and buy him Daddies Sauce. He will show you how he cares if you buy him Daddies Sauce. Well I got him two bottles. Well he was me Daddy, wasn't he? And I was showing him I cared! And not only that, it was a lot cheaper than Heinz. But it did come out of the bottle a lot faster than Heinz, as I found out in rather unexpected circumstances, when we got back to number 11...

Some things were easy to pinch. You can easily put them in your pockets if you got under the mirrors in Jacksons. Things like Oxo cubes and Bisto gravy. The people who worked in Jacksons were always watching us and saying,

'We can see you, you know.'

We had to leave our three boxes and half a dozen carrier bags just inside the entrance of Jacksons where our Bobby would keep not just an eye on our groceries but also an eye out for me. And when he thought the staff weren't looking into the mirrors he'd give me the nod and I'd sneak the oxos and gravy granules into me pocket.

Well as you know? I like Mars bars. And as far as prices were concerned, two boxes of Oxos and one packet of gravy granules equalled three Mars bars. Well me Dad got his Oxos and his gravy granules didn't he? I also saved him money on his Radox and the Daddies Sauce.

He wouldn't know would he? He wasn't going to be bothered about two boxes of Oxos and a box of gravy granules was he? We were soon to find out.

We put the three Mars bars in the shopping basket. That was a big mistake!

'Don't forget the receipt,' our Bobby shouted.

We got everything on the list apart from one thing that had changed its name, the sauce. How we got everything home I will never know. We kept stopping and waiting for each other in the pouring rain. The egg boxes were getting wet. And I had that box. For fuck sake hurry up and let's get home, I said.

The round journey would have been about a quarter of a mile. But you'd have thought it was at least five miles. That walk across the Yorkshire Moors was easier!

But at least we had a Mars bar each. We ate them before we got out of Jacksons. Well 'A Mars A Day...' they used to say. And I believed them. They certainly helped us work, carrying them big heavy boxes - and I mean heavy boxes. But I've never been so sure about the 'rest and play' bit though. We didn't seem to get much opportunity for that!

I still love Mars bars to this day. I like to freeze them so they last longer.

Well we finally all got to the back door at number 11.

Then it was, 'You go in first, Mally.'

We had been out well over an hour with no jackets on. We were all soaking wet through.

Well as soon as we got in the kitchen the old man greeted us with, 'Where the fuck have you three been?'

There we were, soaking wet and struggling with a pile of carrier bags and boxes full of fruit, vegetables and groceries. I felt like saying where the fuck do you think we've been, out playing football, you wanker? But you just couldn't win with the old man. He was always right!

Me Mam though was just the opposite. She made a fuss of us as soon as we got in.

'Come and get warm,' she said. 'Get out of those wet clothes, you'll be catching yer death of cold standing about in them. Quick get the grub away, get it in the pantry.'

She started to empty the boxes but me old man told her to

leave the boxes alone.

'I want to check they've got what I sent them for,' he said.

Well there we all were in the kitchen apart from me old man, that is. The pantry was in the living room where the gas fridge was. That was always a real bastard to light when it went out. It was like harvest festival in our back kitchen. But we had to take one box at a time through into the living room where me Dad was waiting to check them.

He was sitting behind a little wooden coffee table. It was only a small one, but just big enough for him to get his big oval dinner plate on. When me Dad had his dinner he looked just like that giant from the fairy story, 'Jack and the Beanstalk'.

Well there he was in front of us, our own fucking giant! His hands were bigger than the garden shovel. When he went for a handful of coal it was enough to keep the fire going for the full day! You had to have a fire to get a bath in them days.

Well the giant would say, after he'd cleared his table ready for the boxes and he was ready to check everything we had fetched back, and I mean every single thing,

'Right, let's check everything's here! Fetch me that box with all the fruit in,' he'd say.

'Yes Dad,' we'd reply.

Then the giant would say, 'Now fetch me the receipt for all the fruit.'

'Yes Dad,' we'd all say.

He would have his copy of the shopping list in one hand and the receipts in the other.

I was the box carrier. My Mam was waiting in the pantry ready to put the grub away. And Trevor and Bobby formed the chain gang from the old man and me to the pantry.

All the fruit was right. One bunch of bananas, 'Check,' we would say. As it passed through our hands each one of us in turn had to say 'check'. That was the rule. As it dropped into our hands, all the way along to me Mam,

'Check.' - 'Check.' - 'Check.'

If things were going all right, we could hear me Mam singing, 'Check, check, check, check chicken.' That usually made us smile. It did that day as well - until we came to the last box! Everything was 'checking' just fine. The receipts all matched with the shopping list and the giant kept saying, 'Check.'

Everything went well until he said, 'Now bring me the last box.'

'Yes Dad,' we replied. Yes, Daddy, I was thinking. Because the Daddies Sauce and the eggs and the bread were in the last box - not forgetting the custard pies - and the two boxes of Oxos and the box of gravy granules, which I'd stolen and got the three Mars bars instead.

And yes you've guessed it, the Mars bars were of course on the last receipt, he'd bound to notice them!

I guessed he already knew when he asked for the two boxes of Oxos and the box of gravy granules. I saw it in his face when I reached in between the bread and the eggs - and not forgetting the two bottles of Daddies Sauce.

'Two boxes of Oxos and one box of gravy granules,' mumbled me Dad.

'Check,' I said trying to pass them to Trevor very quickly. But Trevor looked a little puzzled and for some reason started to repeat it,

'Two boxes of Oxos and a box of gravy granules, check.'

'Hang on!' the giant growled. 'Those aren't on the receipt!'

'Oh that's good then,' said me Mam quickly, 'they must have got them for nowt. Good lads,' she continued, 'it's about time we had a bit of luck and got something for nothing.'

But me Mam's quick thinking didn't fool me Dad.

'How did you get them?' me Dad asked.

I don't know Dad, I said. The lady might have forgotten to take the money, Dad - Check!

There was a big queue and she was real fast on that new till they have, Dad - Check!

We just put things in the boxes Dad as she said she'd done that basket, Dad - Check!

She's real quick Dad - Check!

'And where does it say three fucking Mars bars on this shopping list?' he bawled.

Thank fuck I was near the back kitchen door!

I felt myself 'frowning'.

I don't know Dad.

'I'll fucking ask you again,' he bawled even louder, 'Why is there two boxes of fucking Oxos and a fucking box of gravy powder on the shopping list and not on the fucking receipt list? Yet three fucking Mars bars are on the fucking receipt, yet not on the fucking shopping list. Why?' he screamed!

Fuck that, I was already edging towards the kitchen door.

Don't know Dad.

'And where's me custard pies?'

He was like fucking Desperate Dan!

They only had one big one and two small ones left Dad.

'What's it say on the list?' he screamed.

Two big custard pies Dad, I replied, why was he always asking me? They only had one big pie left Dad.

'Well what did you get two fucking small ones for then?'

I don't know Dad.

'Why did you get two small ones?' he repeated.

I don't know Dad.

'Who paid for the Mars bars?' he screamed even louder.

Fuck that, I knew what he was doing, he was getting me within arms length. I thought I'm not taking another beating all because of a Mars bar!

'Where's me tomato sauce?'

Oh fuck, here he goes again.

They never had any Dad, so I got you some Daddies Sauce instead.

That was it!

'You fucking what!' he bawled.

With that he bent down and in one fell swoop he lifted his little table up with the big box which had the bread in the bottom and the boxes of eggs and the Daddies Sauce on the top, not forgetting his custard pies. He threw it in the air with all his might, up above my head it flew and then it came crashing down on me. It didn't hurt. It was only bread, eggs and custard pies. But the Daddies Sauce bottle had broken on the ceiling and the sauce was running down my forehead. It was very watery. It looked like blood.

With that me Dad said, 'Now get back to that fucking shop and get me the money back for them fucking Mars bars!'

I didn't need telling twice!

That was my chance to escape. I was out that back door as quick as Batman gets out of his bat cave!

But I wasn't heading back to Jacksons!

Fuck going back there! I didn't know where I was going.

I only knew I was never going back to number 11 ever again. That was it! I just ran - and ran - and ran. I was just running in the rain. Then I was singing in the rain. Then I was dancing in the rain. I was free. I knew then how Rommy had felt when he'd broken free from his lead. That was it! I'd left number 11 with nowt. But I had everything.

I had my freedom. I had the whole world. I had me!

I'd learned some hard lessons from me Dad. Some of them came in handy later as the years rolled by. And as the song went, I was just a lonely boy, lonely and blue. I'm so alone with nothing to do...

That was it! I had nowhere to go. Nobody to turn to. I was out on the streets. But I soon got wise. I had to!

Well what would you have done?

Would you have gone and tried to get the money back from Jacksons? knowing you had no chance. Knowing you'd pinched the Oxos and gravy powder. Knowing there'd be a good beating off the old man whatever the outcome. Or would you just keep running? Well I just kept running.

Fuck that I thought - there was no way I was going back to that!

I just kept running. Crying my eyes out.

Soaking fucking wet. No coat. No money. Nothing.

Nowhere to run to. Nowhere to go!

Fucking egg and tomato sauce running down my head and down me back - not to mention the large custard pie!

Ah! Ah! I thought - at least he wouldn't be having that after his fucking Fray Bentos steak and kidney fucking pies, would he? And his half a loaf of uncut fucking bread, with half a fucking pound of fucking boiled ham. With his tomato fucking sauce spread on his fucking ham.

When he'd fucking swallowed that fucking lot, he'd usually finish by swallowing his fucking custard pie in two fucking bites. Then wash the whole lot down with a mug as big as a fucking bucket, full of fucking tea! But not tonight!

The only thing that whistled in our house was the fucking kettle cos he was always telling us or shouting at us from the garden to come in and turn that fucking thing off!

Me Mam used to call it Billy Boy. She was forever making me Dad a mug of tea.

Well he wouldn't be having that fucking lot that fucking night, would he?

Fuck him I thought! Fuck him! I should have stabbed him when I had the chance, the bastard.

Fucking bastard!

He got his fucking Oxos and that, didn't he?

It was cos we got three fucking Mars bars. All that bother because of three fucking Mars bars!

I wouldn't mind our Trevor and Bobby had a Mars bar each as well. They never said owt. Saying that how could they, they were both shitting themselves!

And I was the nearest the door. I know I would have got it if I'd gone back to number 11.

Fuck that. Our kid would have told me Dad anyway. I didn't blame him for that. But knowing me Dad, he'd already know all about the Mars bars. I just couldn't go back.

Why the fuck me? I was thinking. What have I done wrong?

What the fuck had I done wrong to be born one of eight lads a year between us and I'm the twin. To be born to the most loving mother any child could have wished to have. Who did her very best to cope with the life she had.

She was my pal of my cradle days. She was a Dame. She was a Queen. She was my Queen. But there I was running away from her. Leaving her with that evil, mad bastard.

If only you knew what that felt like! What would you have done? I was only fifteen years of age.

I'd been thrown through a glass window at five years of age. Put in that 'nice' house in Sutton where you could hear the other lads screaming for their Mams in the night, in that strange sort of way, No, Sir! No, Sir!! Punched off a little bike in hospital which gave me another week in there, hospital that was. Then punched from wall to wall for 'frowning'. Then fucking battered to fuck when me Dad thought I had pinched that ten bob note off that lass at the fair. And forced to drink half a glass of Lamb's Navy Rum after he'd beaten me fucking black and blue. Fuck that! That was for something I never did.

Then there was the beating I got for standing up to the fucking school bully! Fuck that as well! What was he going to do to me for something I actually did? Pinching the Mars bars.

There was no way I was going back to find out. Fuck it! I'd had enough! Soaking fucking wet, crying, what for? Why was I crying? Then I realised. That was it.

There was no turning back. My whole life had changed.

That was it!

No turning back! I was out. I was free. I should have been happy. But I wasn't happy. I was mad! I was angry. I was lost. Lost in the wilderness.

Why me? Why the fucking hell me?

Well I'm glad he never got his fucking custard pie!

Well there's nothing wrong with a bit of black humour, now and again. And he did used to call this six-foot olive skinned kid, 'you little black bastard'.

I might as well have been a bastard cos there's no way he was ever much of a father to me. Dads don't do that to their sons, do they? What would you have done in my shoes? I'll tell you exactly what I did!

Nobody wanted me. I had nobody to turn to.

I didn't know where my older brothers lived and I didn't know them that well anyway.

Our Richard was living at his girlfriend's house. But I didn't know where any of the others were. I knew our David had gone to sea. I got to know him later in life.

I didn't know where the others where. But I knew where the fish docks were. Cos I used to go meet the trawlers when they came home from sea. When the ship came alongside the quay we'd help the fishermen with their kit bags and they'd give us a back-hander - money - for our help.

The fishermen were always happy and smiling and singing. They were happy to be home. So why the fuck wasn't my Dad ever happy when he came home?

Well to get onto the docks you had to run across the railway lines cos there was always a copper at the foot of the bridge at the bottom of Liverpool Street. That was one of only two entrances to the dock, the other being at the town end.

And that copper would not let you on unless you had a job on the docks.

You know - bobbing - unloading the ships. Filleting - boning and cutting up the fish. Barrow boy - fetching and carrying the fish on a two-wheeled barrow.

I loved that job when I finally got it. But first I had to find somewhere to stay. I was still soaking wet remember.

Well over them railway lines there used to be a load of old, derelict concrete air-raid shelters. The fish merchants used to store boxes and old wooden benches in them shit holes.

The buildings were warm but overrun with rats - but they wouldn't hurt you, would they?

At least that's what I remember me old man saying when he told us, 'Go kill that rat in that trap.'

But nine times out of ten when you opened the trap the rat would be that quick, it would be out and over your hands and away. Sometimes it would run up your arms. Arrgghh!!

So I believed if a rat saw you it would run away. And what your eyes don't see when you're asleep can't hurt you can it?

Sommat like that isn't it? Same as what the eyes don't see the heart can't grieve. What a load of bollocks that saying is. What the eyes can't see the heart can't grieve?

The times I was in that bomb shelter on that dock on a night and crying for me Mam. Crying for my dear Mother. Crying because I knew what she would be going through at number 11. Thank fuck I'd escaped...

I soon got a job as a barrow boy. Those barrows had two thick rubber wheels coated with a metal casing. The wheels were about a foot in diameter. Heavy wheels they were. Then you had the handles that were about four feet high and about two feet wide at the bottom coming up to about a foot wide at the top. It was hard to get yer grip a foot wide.

Then at the bottom of the barrow was a thick metal plate about two foot wide made from very heavy metal plate, about three inches thick. It was one heavy beast but you had to be able to push it with about ten stones of fish in an aluminium kit which the bobbers had filled from that trawler that had landed her catch the night before. Sometimes five or six ships used to land together with each ship landing up to 2,000 kits of fish on that 'half a mile market'.

If the firm that you worked for had bought 50 kits of fish at the far end of the market, it was your job to go and fetch it to the men at the other end so they could fillet them. That could easily take you all morning, running backwards and forwards starting at six o'clock. Well I was never late of course cos it was only twenty yards across the road to my 'bunker'. And the gaffer used to wake me up at half past five in the morning, every morning, to take me for a 'big breakfast' at Stanton's Café, which was situated in between two docks. St Andrews Dock was used for landing the deep-sea trawlers and Albert Dock handled all the inshore boats, from places such as Scarborough and Bridlington.

Whenever old man Stanton saw my boss Stan and me come into his café, he'd always welcome us in the same way.

'Two well-buttered bread cakes for him and whatever the lad wants - and double up because Stan's paying,' he shouted to whoever was frying. Then while we were waiting for that full breakfast, old man Stanton would say to me,

'Go and get a wash and tidy yourself up a bit.'

He had a sink in the back and I'd go in there and get a wash, dreading to look in the mirror because of all the spots I had.

My boss, Stan, had bought me a toothbrush and toothpaste and some soap. I used Stanton's towel.

By the time I'd had a good wash and brush up, the big breakfast would be waiting.

Two eggs, four rashers of bacon, four sausages, fried bread, mushrooms, beans, tomatoes, four slices of toast and a big mug of tea. And guess which sauce was on the table? Yes, it was always - Daddies!

'There you go my lad, get plenty of that sauce on it, it will kill the taste,' joked old man Stanton.

Then he'd say, 'Go on my lad show them how you can eat.'

And when I tucked into that breakfast all I thought of was, our Trevor and Bobby wouldn't be having this.

Fuck them anyway. If they want to stop at number 11, that was their choice! I'd chosen to leave...

My first job each day was to take all the fish Stan bought to our stand so the men could fillet it.

As I say that could sometimes take me all morning because they started selling the fish at seven in the morning so I had to be ready just in case my boss bought early.

The docks were like an ant colony. The buzz was great and I loved working there. And my boss always paid me double what the other barrow boys were getting.

Do you know why?

'Because you are the best barrow boy in this town,' he would say. And there were about 100 of us on the docks at the time I was down there. But hey, I loved the work-out.

By it was hard work, but I loved it!

I was getting my meals - doing something I loved - and getting twice as much as the other barrow boys.

When I'd got all the fish up to the stand, Stan used to say to me, 'Go fill yer face up at Stanton's.' That meant it was time for my dinner. 'But make sure you're back in two hours.' That was because all the fish had to go in two stone wooden boxes filled with ice and we had to nail the wooden lids on as well. Then load our barrows up and take them to the wagons that would go and deliver our fish to our customers.

Sometimes we would carry about 30 stone of fish on that barrow, it was all about balance. Once you'd loaded up your barrow and had got it balanced, once you got into your stride, your trot, then the canter, it was magic once you got into your gallop, you were away...

The one thing we didn't want was anybody pinching our fish. And there were a lot of 'dodgy' people who worked on them docks. But I soon found out how I could 'earn' extra money doing exactly that! I was soon earning more than the men that worked there. Three times as much...

Fuck staying in that shit hole, that poxy air-raid shelter. I wanted a flat. So I started to save me money up for one. But I was only fifteen and a half years old.

As soon as I finished my work on the docks I would go to Madley Street Baths for a good soak. When you'd done a full day's graft on that dock all you wanted was that nice hot bath. Madley Street was just off the docks. The quickest way to get there was over them railway lines. So you had to pass that copper at the bridge. I remember a copper called Shuffler. He was one of the nice coppers. Don't get me wrong, he wasn't afraid to give you that clip, especially when he caught you dropping spunk balls on the other barrow lads' heads.

What are 'spunk balls' I hear you say. Let me explain.

The dog fish which looked like small sharks used to have these big bags of milky fluid inside them. And if you burst them - did they smell?

Well the filleters used to put them in the 'shit tub' very gently of course because if you burst them they would stink - what a weapon - those spunk balls.

The barrow boys used to collect those spunk balls and put them in their plastic bread bags.

Well the docks used to have shall we call it a second floor above where the men were filleting - what a weapon those spunk balls were.

Well most barrow lads used to go upstairs so to speak after their morning's work and after dinner.

The quicker you got your fish to your stand the longer you had for your dinner and the longer you had upstairs playing football, rugby or cricket. You could have even had a nine hole golf course up there, it was that big upstairs. By I had loads of fights up there! Remember I was the best barrow lad on the dock, even with my fists.

Well, spunk balls at the ready! Find out where that wanker was working. You know, that clever wanker that had just started on the docks that day. Hundreds came and went, barrow boys that was, half of them couldn't push an empty barrow, never mind one with thirty stones of fish on it!

Well the new lads used to get it like we all got it when we first started - the spunk balls that was. The spunk balls. Wait till that person was right underneath you and you were 30 foot above them, spunk bag at the ready.

5-4-3-2-1 Bombs away!

Bingo! Take that yer tosser!

That's where the saying came from, 'Emptying yer ball bag'!

Half the time the people, whether man or boy, didn't know who'd done it - but Shuffler did! He had his informers. And Shuffler would creep up on yer, hence his name Shuffler. Then he would give you that clip after you had just emptied yer ball bag. But it was nowt like the clip what the old man gave me. It was just that tender clip round yer lugs!

I used to love it on that market, especially when a load of dogfish got landed. I got someones ball bag emptied on me and to this day I still don't know who it was. But hey, it was just a prank. I loved it. I was beginning to laugh again.

Well that bath at Madley Street came in very handy especially on days like that. And it made things even better when you knew the bath attendant liked fish. No problems there. Some fish for a bath!

Well for a good three months I slept in that rat hole until Shuffler finally caught me crossing them railway lines one night. I was just coming back from the youth club.

Oh yes, Sidney Smith youth club - those were the days!

That's where I met the mother of my only son, Peter.

Her name was Karen. She was the best looking lass at that youth club, in my eyes. I always said she looked like the singer, Kate Bush. I used to go to the club just to see her. Believe it or not, I was very shy where girls were concerned at that stage of my life.

Well I hadn't been through much mixed schooling apart from two or three years when I started at Francis Askew. And at that age my tail was just for pissing out of. I didn't know that girls were very different to boys. Girls? if you talked to girls you were a sissy when you were seven or eight years old! Then all that time away spent only with other boys and at fifteen and a half years of age I still didn't have much of a clue what my 'piss-prodder' was for. But I was soon to find out, even though I was still covered in acne!

Well I always stood in the dark at the youth club when it was 'Disco Nights'. What I had to do to hide them fucking spots. And before the lights came on at the end of the dancing - I was off! That was until I met Karen Roberts, my Kate Bush look-alike!

Karen was soon to become the mother of my one and only boy, Peter. I also need to tell you I now have two daughters Tammie and Keelie to my ex-wife Kerry. And not forgetting my two grandsons, Kailem and Aydan.

I'll tell you in chapter ten what happened that night when Shuffler caught me crossing them railway lines and about those unforgettable nights at the youth club.

My time when Karen's Mam and Dad took me in - away from my 'bunker'.

Then the birth of my son. And my first trip to sea.

Oh, and let's not forget my first flat - my first real home!

So I hope the picture I'm painting is a good one. I was happy. Happy until I saw me Dad, that is!

Just when I thought it was all over...

I used to go and see me Mam and take her some cigs and

hairspray when me Dad was away.

But there was a time when I thought he was away and I went through the back door at number 11 and I was greeted with, 'What the fuck are you doing here?

It was the giant!

And in the next chapter I'll tell you more about how I slept in a concrete shelter on the docks. How I met my son's mother. What happened when I made my first trip to sea. And how I got my first proper little home and then made the mistake of letting our Trevor and Bobby move in with me.

See you in ten!

Mally

CHAPTER TEN
YOU'RE THE FIRST, THE LAST, MY EVERYTHING

Love lifted me up where I belonged. Well, Karen did!

You'll notice all of my chapters are headed with song titles, or lines from songs. Well life's a song isn't it? And life can be a bit of a 'mind boggle' can't it?

Which brings me back to the present day.

We all listen to music don't we? And when we hear that certain song - how it fetches back those memories.

Well I go through life now singing them old songs - those golden oldies - that they play on our local radio station, BBC Radio Humberside. And every record they play brings back a memory for me!

Well you know how popular the music from the sixties and the seventies still is.

Well that was 'my' music! And I still love it and dance and sing along to it every day.

I can remember buying my first record for Karen. It was 'You're The First, The Last, My Everything' by Barry White. It got to number one in November 1974. I was sixteen and I loved it!

Well if you know what it was like in the early seventies, we used to buy records all the time. I know I did for Karen. I think I used to buy her about one every week.

She was into the 'Bay City Rollers'. Oh, how we sang 'Shang-A-Lang' as we ran with the gang. I used to be into Gary Glitter. Do You Want To Be In My Gang? Perhaps I shouldn't dwell too much on Gary after recent events.

Then there was Slade, oh yeah and Abba!

So I'll tell you about Karen by using all those great songs we used to listen to.

The same way as I did on the Paul Hartley Show on BBC Radio Humberside 95.9FM. I never used to listen to Radio Humberside till I was going down Hedon Road in my wagon

one day. I was bouncing in and out of the pot-holes in the road
- long before it was all widened to a dual carriageway - and I
lost the station I was tuned into. And as I was trying to retune
to what I'd been listening to I came across what I later found
out to be the 'Paul Hartley Show'. He was having a phone-in
quiz where he gave you the answer and you had to ring in and
provide the question.

The answer that day was 'sand'.

Well you just had to phone the radio station, speak to Paul for
a couple of minutes, then give him your answer and hope it
was the one he was looking for.

Well I got through to the show and I was 'live' on air. Bear in
mind I'd never rang into a radio station before. Well I was on
for a good ten minutes and believe me we had a good laugh,
which we still do to this day.

Paul's a great guy with a wicked sense of humour and he plays
them golden oldies and great music.

Well anyway the question to the answer, sand, if you see what
I mean, which I gave him was, What goes with gravel, cement
and water to make concrete?

To fill them pot-holes on Hedon Road, what the Council had
forgotten to repair. Which had just cost me a new exhaust, I
told him.

Well to my amazement it was the answer he was looking for!
I'd won! Two tickets to go to see Status Quo!

Well from that day on, I have Radio Humberside on from the
moment I get up to going to bed every day of the week. I'm a
regular on Paul's show. I love it when I get on air with Paul.

Well, he also had this other game called 'The Music Mind
Boggler' where he gave you a song title and you had to get to
another song of your choice by using all other song titles,
linking each song to each other.

You'll get the idea as we go along.

Because I want to tell you in song titles and links about the
time I was head over heels in love with Karen. And about
when I first met her at the tender age of sixteen...

She came on like a dream, peaches and cream, lips like
strawberry wine. She was sixteen, she was beautiful, she was
mine! Well I said to her, You're my first, you're my last, you're
my everything.

YOU'RE THE FIRST, THE LAST, MY EVERYTHING

Slade used to say, Girls grab the boys, Karen used to say, let's dance, yeah, Chris Montez!

And I said, Mamma Mia, here we go again, my my, how could I resist her?

Then, I want to hold your hand - and when I touched her I felt happy inside, it's such a feeling that my love I can't hide.

She made me feel like dancing, yeah Leo Sayer!

Karen did look a lot like Kate Bush. We did reach those Wuthering Heights and we also went running up that hill!

Young love, first love, we'll share with deep emotions, said Donny Osmond. His brothers sang about those Crazy Horses and little Jimmy was that Long haired lover from Liverpool. Donny also did the twelfth of never.

And I used to say to Karen, I'm never gonna give you up, never gonna let you down, that would be until the twelfth of never, I thought. All I wanted was for her to love me tender, love me true, tell me you'll be mine - Elvis - I've done the jailhouse rock, I'll tell you about that later.

We all get suspicious minds don't we?

My all time favourite song to this day has to be, When no one else can understand me, when everything I do is wrong, you give me hope and inspiration, you give me strength to carry on, I guess I'll never know the reason why you love me like you do, I guess that's the wonder, the wonder of you.

Well, everyone considered me the coward of the county - the youth club in my case - when I tried to say no to the fights! Then it was bang bang, they hit the ground, bang bang, that awful sound, bang bang, when I knocked them down! I was not the coward of the county!

Oh, we'd get the blanket from the bedroom, and we'd go walking once again - to her garage - and I would say lay back in the arms of someone you love, and then I kissed her.

She was in my heart and in my soul, I thought she'd be my breath till I grew old, nice one Rod!

Well love really hurt without you, I'd sing.

Well after all, Karen was my first, my last, my everything.

Or so I thought! And hey if you happen to see the most beautiful girl in the world, tell her I'm sorry!

Cos I remember April when the sun was in the sky and love was burning in your eyes, nothing in the world could bother me, I was living in a world of make believe. And now she's gone I'm just a daydreamer - David Cassidy - he made a comeback didn't he?

Oh we did the kissing in the back rows - tenfoots - and people used to say to Karen, he's a rebel and he'll never, ever be any good. He's a rebel and he'll never, ever do what he should.

Well I had to do things my way, let's be Frank!

Then I had to run for home, run as fast as I can, to get across them railway lines, to my rat-infested, shit hole of an air raid shelter before Shuffler the copper did his night shift.

Well that night Shuffler caught me in my 'den' and arrested me. I spent the night in his office, pleading with him not to get in touch with my Mam and Dad. Please, I was begging him. And a bit to my surprise he never did. Because he knew all about big, bad John.

We had to wait until Stan my boss turned up at 5.30 the next morning to sort things out. Stan said he would make sure I never slept in that shit hole ever again. And he did.

'From now on you can stay in that spare office,' he said.

By it was nice and warm compared with the shit hole. A bit like what I'm in at the moment, I'll tell you about that later...

I was in love at sixteen years of age and how could you tell? Easy - I was carrying fifty stone of fish instead of that thirty stone. I just wanted to spend more time with the girl I was in love with.

I would be at the baths every day. So I had to get more fish. I think all the lads off the dock were paying in fish. That baths' attendant could have opened his own 'chippy' with the amount we used to give him.

I just couldn't wait to hold Karen's hand and kiss the most beautiful girl from the youth club. We once kissed for a full hour without our lips parting. A full hour, that takes some doing. But not with these lucky lips, may I say.

Well my mother did say I had lucky lips - Cliff Richard. When I was sat on her knee she used to put her hand gently over my face - maybe she didn't want to squeeze my spots.

I can remember on one of them occasions when me Mam said, 'Oh Mally, you are going to break them women's hearts - you have lucky lips - and when your spots go, you're going to be a real heartbreaker. You're going to be one handsome man when you grow up. And promise me that when you hit someone, you won't hit them too hard.'

If only I'd taken me Mam's advice all them years ago. Who knows I may never have gone to prison. I'll tell you about my spells in prison as we go along.

Oh one other thing my Mam told me was, Son you'll be a bachelor boy and that's the way you'll stay - Cliff again!

But walk tall, walk straight and look the world right in the eye. See what I mean about songs? You can't speak without a song coming to you.

Well anyway Paul on the radio doesn't do the 'mind boggler' anymore. But I used to love it. It was my daily 'fix' during the week. I will tell you the 'mind boggler' I did when I got on his show. I told him in song titles how I got through to the last stages of the TV programme, 'Big Brother'.

Yer, I'm not shy no more! I'm catching up on what I've missed out on in life - and that's laughter!

I hope my humour is coming across OK. It's taken me all this time to come out of my shell. Because I used to be very, very, shy. Cos as you may have gathered I was brought up in a very repressed environment.

I was brought up in that 'male environment'.

Just think about it. Eight brothers. Then all boy's children's homes. Then boy's approved schools. Boy's detention centre. Male borstal. All male prison. And all male fishing industry.

So you can imagine what it was like for this six-foot, spotty faced sixteen-year-old when I met the most beautiful girl that I'd ever seen - and fell head over heels in love with her! But then I lost her love...

Oh yes, I was in love with Karen OK. But the problem was I was sixteen and sleeping in a spare office on the docks. Well it was somewhere to get yer head down - and I was on the job, so to speak. But it wasn't what I wanted...

I soon learnt how to earn some extra cash, on top of what I was getting off Stan, my boss. Bear in mind, I was getting finished as early as possible. With my job you know, barrowing the fish what Stan had bought.

I was the best barrow lad on the dock so they told me. But it was just a good way of keeping fit and getting even fitter at the same time. It was a piece of piss really.

MALLY - THE BOY WHO FLEW THROUGH WINDOWS

The market was sometimes full of kits of fish and on some occasions they were blocking the access to the fish-filleters. We had to move those ten-stone kits of fish in them aluminium, opened barrels on our barrows, which by the way had our names engraved on the handle.

My name was on the longest.

After a lot of practise we also learned to roll the kits of fish with two hands. And once we'd got the knack of that we soon learned to roll the kit with one hand while the other hand was milking the kit of fish - taking a fish out of the kit as we rolled it. We only took fish out of the kits that did not belong to us.

Nine times out of ten the big boys - the likes of Birds Eye, Findus, Marrs, Smales etc. - would buy all the fish on the market. They'd send big wagons and park outside your stand and two men would come and clear the fish that their company had bought that day. And what little fish that was left, the small boys would have to pay higher prices for. Not much has changed in life, the big boys get what they want, fuck the small man - business that is.

Well when the likes of Birds Eye bought all the fish that was on the market, there was very little fish for the other fish merchants.

Well that full-time job became part-time. The times we never got any fish started to get more than when we did get fish. And you had to make your money up somehow!

And as I say I soon learnt how to hand roll these kits of fish. In the end I joined that elite group that could spin that kit of fish - it was all about balance.

The knack of rolling and spinning them kits gave you that spare hand that allowed you to 'milk' the kit of fish!

You only needed to take one fish out of each kit, which would accidentally fall out while you were helping to clear the market for the big boys - without any pay - greedy bastards!

When the fish fell out with a little help from my spare hand, I would give it the back flip with my size thirteen clogs. And the fish would slide under a filleting bench, awaiting me to go back to my little haul when they cleared the fish off our stand. Well I also soon learnt how to fillet fish, in a ragger's sort of way. I wasn't a good filleter. I still aren't. I would be classed as a ragger in the filleting game today, but I soon learnt how to fillet, I took my time because I had the time. Cos as I say I lived on the job so to speak. The times I had about forty stone of fish to fillet, well I needed the money for that flat that I wanted. Because I didn't want to stay in that one roomed office, even if it was warm, did I?

Karen came from a loving home - very different to mine!

And the day soon came when I got to meet her Mam and Dad. I took to Audrey and Roy straight away.

Oh she was a lovely lady was Audrey. She must have been to that same loving school that my Mam went to. And Roy, Karen's Dad was a real gentleman. A gentle man. Not like me old man!

I used to get Audrey and Roy lots of fish. I used to love going to Karen's house for tea and Sunday lunch. Roy and Audrey took me as they found me.

Roy had a 'wandering' eye, a 'lazy' eye. He'd be reading the paper but you'd think he was looking at you. I'd be trying to touch Karen or give her a kiss and his eye would wander across and I'd stop cos I thought he was looking at us - but he never was.

Roy was a great guy. He was more of a father to me than my own Dad ever was. I'll always thank him for that.

And Audrey was my second Mother. No other woman could replace my Mam of course. But Audrey came a close second at that time in my life.

Karen's Mam would say,

'Fetch your washing and I'll wash it for you.'

It all happened over thirty years ago now. How times fly. Thirty years ago. It's frightening sometimes how quickly time passes isn't it?

But sometimes life can also seem to go slowly. Especially when you're in prison, which was to come. And all those lonely nights at sea, especially when you get the 'thinks' on.

Tell you about some of the 'thinks' as we go along. They can really do your head in when you're away from the ones you love. And you start to think about them. And you can't do nowt about it when you have the 'thinks' on!

The times I had the 'thinks' on when I was at sea, in prison, or in that little office on the docks. I still get the 'thinks' on sometimes, but not 'stinking thinking'.

Well I had to sleep in that shit hole on the docks for about another six months. Then one day Karen's Mam and Dad asked if I wanted to stay with them. They knew I was sleeping on the docks.

I can remember the time very well because Karen had missed her monthly - and I'm not talking about a magazine.

I also remember exactly when and where Peter was conceived. It happened down the tenfoot at the back of the garages. I didn't really know what my 'equipment' was for when I was sixteen. But it was that kiss. Once I got that kiss. And those sexual feelings took over. That was it!

But within thirty seconds it was all over. I'd finished. I didn't even know that either! But within a few weeks, Karen told me she was pregnant!

She was only sixteen when she had Peter. And trying to hide it from her Mam - the whole thing was unbelievable.

I met her again at me Son's wedding - we reminisced and had a good chat - but that's later on...

Things on the fish dock were going fairly quiet. The big boys were buying all the fish up. I didn't want to work in a factory. How could you get a flat on the money they were paying for factory work? And on top of that my girlfriend was having my baby. How strange - and we dared not tell her Mam and Dad.

Roy used to work in an engineering business. He said he could get me a job there if I fancied it but I didn't want to do that.

Karen also had two brothers and a sister - and I was living with them. I slept in the same room as Karen's older brother Kevin. She also had a younger brother, Billy, and a younger sister. But as much as I loved Roy and Audrey and Karen's family, including her Nanna who lived on First Lane, Hessle, I just had to get us a place of our own.

The only way I was going to get enough money to get out of Karen's loving but overcrowded home was to go to sea on the trawlers. Karen didn't want me to go to sea. She didn't want me to go away three weeks at a time - she wanted me there with her. But everything was strange to me. I was missing my Mother. And even though I got the motherly love of Audrey, it wasn't the same. I just wanted to go to sea.

Oh I worked in a scrapyard - you know scrap cars and that - but I think the sea was in my blood. It was not only in my blood, it became my life for the next fifteen years. And it led me to the detention centre and then to prison...

Well it wasn't much later that we realised Karen just couldn't hide the fact that she was pregnant any longer. Bear in mind Karen was only sixteen and I wasn't much older. And that thirty years ago things were very different. What would the neighbours think?

Karen used to go out with this other lad - they were just friends. He used to live opposite her. He was the best looking lad who used to go to the youth club, bastard! I can laugh about it now, but back then I thought the good looking bastard, go and find someone else!

He'd always fancied Karen. He was always sniffing around. Well she was the best looking lass at the youth club. The times me and Karen would argue over him. I guess it was just my insecurity! Well I was only sixteen, put yourself in my place! There I was with my first love and this creep sniffing round my girlfriend. Every time I went round to her house this good looking bastard was there. He wouldn't stand a chance nowadays, not with this Prince amongst men. Oh he was a real slime-ball!

The times I remember being in that shed on that dock thinking about that slime-ball talking to my girlfriend.

Well he only lived on the other side of the street to her, bastard! Well I'm sure you can picture it, what would you have done? He was a fucking slime-ball - and a good-looking one at that!

I'm sure we can all relate to meeting a slime-ball in life.

I've met loads in business - I'll tell you more about them as we go along. I know I'm bouncing backwards and forwards a bit at times but I just type it as it comes to me.

What I'm trying to say is that I really loved this girl. And this fucking slime-ball was trying to get her to go out with him.

Maybe because she could kiss for a whole hour without stopping. But she only did that with me, I hope. Nobody was going to get that. That was mine!

I can still see him now while I'm typing, the fucking snaky bastard. The times I sat in that shit hole on the dock. Thinking. Thinking. Thinking. There were times when I would get the thinks on and just couldn't shake them off. They wouldn't go away! The times I just wanted to say hey why don't you just fuck off and go and find someone else to talk to, she's my girlfriend!

I just wanted to bang him! But his Mam was Audrey's best friend. It used to tear me apart.

I know but I was only sixteen at the time and on top of that as one spot went another one took its place. Fuck me my face was worse than a spotty dick pudding!

I was a very, very, insecure person.

I blame my old man for that. I had no confidence in front of lasses at that time of my life. To be perfectly truthful, I had no confidence in front of most people.

How times have changed.

Only if you want them to change. You have got to want it and I have changed.

It's taken me over forty years to change but as I say, it's never too late.

But I could do nowt to change how this good-looking kid was sniffing round my girlfriend.

I just had to get to sea. Get away. If not I think I would have battered him. And I couldn't do that because I cared for Audrey and Roy. I didn't want to fetch shame on their doorstep - and on top of that Karen was having my baby. It was one of the few times my 'punch first - ask questions later' motto had to be shelved...

One of my best mates Terry Milner had gone to sea. And when he came home I asked him how I could get to go.

He told me I'd have to go to a fishing school. It was down Boulevard, off Hessle Road.

I think you had to go for about three months to learn the basics. How to get into a life raft - that always stuck with me - you what!

And after you saw some of the films of the trawlers, fishing in them storm force seas, I thought twice about going to sea at all. They were frightening! I think they showed you them just to 'shit you up'.

My elder brother, David, had gone to that school as had my cousins, Ted, Alan, Pete, Andy and Christopher, God rest his soul.

About 20% got through, one out of every five who tried, and

were then placed with a fishing company. The company I was allotted to was called Thomas Hamlyn with those ships named after Saints...

Before you could go to sea you first had to go to a prep school and learn all about the health and safety side of fishing. Then after you'd done three trips you were allowed to work on the deck. And when you'd done six trips on the deck you were allowed to go for your spare hands ticket, then you'd go to a school where you'd learn how to net mend, how to read a compass, learn your signals, the Morse code, etc. etc. Then after another eighteen months to two years you were allowed to go for your bosun's ticket, which I got. That was all about navigation - I got 99.9% on a radar observer's course! - I'm proud about that. I missed the 100% on the thickness of a pencil! Always keep your pencil sharp!

I remember you also had to see the doctor before you could go to sea. When you went to see him he would check your eyesight. Then it would be 'drop and cough'. That was drop yer pants and then cough. So there you were, with yer pants down around yer ankles and yer legs apart. The doctor would put his ice-cold hands on yer testicles and then grab one of yer balls. 'Cough!' he then instructed. Then he'd do the same thing with yer other knacker - how strange!

Then he would say, 'Touch your toes.' That was while yer pants were still down.

Hop on one leg. Then the other. Then he asked,

'Are you fit enough to go to sea?'

And you'd answer, 'Yes Sir!'

Then he'd sign sommat that you had to take to the ship's runner. His name was Renee.

He was a nice guy. I remember him saying,

'Look son, you have to be tough to go to sea, it's a very hard life. They're very tough men who go to sea. You have to look after yourself and behave yourself. If you do, you'll go far!

You will have to work in the ship's galley for the first three trips and if you like it we will let you work on the deck.'

Yes Sir, no problem, I said.

'Fine', he replied, 'Now sign on here - you're going away in two days.'

Only two days and I'd be aboard the St Dominic - and I

hadn't told Karen I was even planning on going yet!

Two days away from my first trip to sea. I was going away. I was going fishing! I was going to get loads of money. I was going to get a flat. Our flat. How I wanted to get that flat. It's all I wanted. A place I could call home. And know that someone was there for me when I got through that door. Someone who loved me. Someone who was having my baby. I would get that flat and get the love of my life to move in with me. And we'd be happy ever after. Sorted! So I thought.

After all I couldn't spend my wages when I was at sea. And I got good money on the trawlers - that's all I wanted to do.

I had two days to get all my gear ready. Just two days!

Two days and I would be going to sea.

Two days and I was going on that journey. A journey that took me down the wrong roads in life.

The life of a fisherman.

The life of boozing and fighting.

The life of fighting every time I came home!

The life of 'The King of the Road.'

The life of being an arsehole!

The Lambs Navy Rum life!

The life I wasted.

I know what they mean when they say, 'If I could only turn back time.' Cher sang that years later, well there were many times when I thought if I could only turn back time.

I wouldn't have acted like I did when I got home from sea. I wouldn't have been out drinking every day and night. And going round to Karen's house and seeing that slime-ball holding my baby.

Yes, if we could only turn back time - and if we knew then, what we know today. We could maybe have changed things.

We were drifting apart. I suppose deep down I knew things weren't going well. And as time went by they got worse.

Whenever I saw him I just saw the red mist! I kept seeing him at the door. I kept seeing him at the back door. I kept seeing him sat in the house. And it was just constantly doing my head in that this slime-ball was sniffing round her.

Later, when I was away at sea, I used to get the 'thinks' on. It was horrible. Lying there in my bed, stuck in the middle of the Atlantic Ocean, thinking what was going on?

YOU'RE THE FIRST, THE LAST, MY EVERYTHING

Who was Karen with? Is the slime-ball with her?

I came home after one trip and got drunk and then went round there and tried to be clever, knocked on his door and told him to stay away from my girlfriend.

Every time I came home from sea, the slime-ball was there! He was always sniffing around. I was going away for three weeks at a time. So I was only on the scene for a week or so once every month. And every time I got home, he would be either sat in her house, or walking her down the street or at the youth club with her. Everywhere I looked he was there. On one occasion he was even holding hands with her! And I thought I'm getting 'shit on' here!

The next thing I knew, the baby was born. And I went round and the slimey bastard was holding my baby in his slimey hands.

Then I got the 'magic' words, He's not yours, he's not yours!

I took it as he wasn't mine. That Peter wasn't my baby. And not what Karen really meant that he wasn't only mine.

So what was I to do? I just went.

Karen had been my first love - it was young love, first love. But it was me that changed.

I started to get the taste for that booze. And when I drank that Lambs Navy Rum, get out of my way! I don't know why but when I drank that stuff that was it. I turned into someone else! The Jeckyll and Hyde came out of me!

Or was it me Dad? Was I acting like me Dad? Or was I actually turning into me Dad?

My first trip to sea was also the last trip to sea for one man.

He threw himself over the side of the ship when we were one day from home on my very first trip to sea. What an introduction to life at sea that was!

They said he owed someone some money and that he thought the police would be waiting for him when we got back to Hull. But they weren't. He went over the side, ended it for nothing! What a waste of a life!

I'll tell you more in chapter eleven about what happened when I first went to sea. How Karen took it. How I lost her love all through alcohol. Yes alcohol, that innocent looking bottle. How I lost the girl I loved through booze and my aggressive behaviour! And about the day she told me it was all over...

It's all in chapter 11. Oh number 11!
There just had to be 11 chapters, didn't there?
Can't forget that number, can I?
The same as I'll never forget how me and Karen parted.
Number 11. Eyes down.
Both the ones. Mally and Trevor.
Number 11! Next to Tony's den.
See yer in 11 - Cheers Mally

CHAPTER ELEVEN
BREAKING UP IS HARD TO DO

Well, they say breaking up is hard to do, don't they?

Well, My bags were packed, I was ready to go, I was standing outside Karen's door, I hate to say goodbye. The taxi was waiting - he was blowing his horn. It was a heartache.

It always was!

Leaving the one you love behind, never knowing if you were to return. Well, you heard of trawlers going away, never to return.

They also say, 'Never look back when you have said your goodbyes.'

These were some of the superstitions. Never wear green. Never let a woman 'set you away to your ship'. By that I mean don't let them come down to the quay to see you off. Say your goodbyes at the door and don't ever look back.

Never look at a cross-eyed man. They said that was unlucky as well. I still think it is unlucky if you look into the eyes of a cross-eyed man. I've nowt against them, cross-eyed men that is. But saying that I won't look at one if I'm having a bet on the horses!

Karen was crying. I was crying. The taxi driver was shouting: 'Come on son we have got to pick the others up. We don't want to miss the tide. Come on, give her a kiss - and don't look back.'

I was going on my first trip to sea on the trawler with the biggest funnel of all the trawlers in the fleet, 'The St Dominic'. But how could I leave the one I loved? The girl that was having my baby. That most gorgeous girl that I had fell in love with?

It was obvious! I wanted that flat, it was our only chance, get to sea, get some money, get that flat and provide for my girlfriend and child. But you know what they say, 'You're too young!'

And how do you feel? You're in the hands of your elders who are still trying to run your life for you.

Most if not all my early years, I was controlled by my elders. What elders? My old man, yes I can thank him for all them beatings.

Toughening me up! Thanks a lot Dad because after taking a beating off me Dad, there was never going to be any man big enough to knock me down again.

That was my outlook.

Why did me Dad give me them severe beatings and not my twin brother?

I don't know. I'll probably never know, until the day I die.

Why did I go to that children's home away from my loving mother, why?

I know some said it was just for our own safety.

I certainly wasn't the one to argue with that assessment with an old man like mine in the house, was I?

And yes I had to agree my Mam couldn't cope, especially later on when she was ill!

But hey, what modern day Mother could cope with eight boys to bring up? And then losing her only daughter in a fire. Come to think of it, what man could cope?

I now try and understand the meaning of it all. But it hurts to recall some of the things that I saw when I was young.

They are some of the things I'd prefer to bury and forget about. To lock them away and never think of them again. But that of course is impossible. Those things are with me forever, I'll never forget them!

The elders, mainly men, in them children's homes. The elders, mainly men, in the approved school. Yes, you hope to learn from them. But some of the things I learned about them, no-one should ever have to know!

I thank a few men that helped me along the way in my early life. The ones that spring to mind are Mr Hall from Stockton Hall Approved School. He taught me how to use the sporting talent I'd been given. He turned me into a very good goalkeeper at the tender age of just 11. He was a true gentleman and a true sportsman.

Roy, Karen's Dad, was another gentleman.

Renee, the ship's runner, the man that told me what the life of a fisherman was going to be like. And let's not forget Stan Cook, the fish merchant who gave me my first job on the docks when I'd run away from number 11 and was lost and alone in that big wilderness.

There are other men who have helped me along this path what I'm on but I will name them as we go along. But one who I must mention, a man I always looked up to, was Arthur Ball. The hours I spent learning from that great skipper made life worthwhile and I loved sailing with him. As far as I was concerned he was the Daddy of skippers.

My first trip to sea was on the sidewinder trawler, called the St Dominic. I think there'd be between thirty to forty trawlers sailing out of Hull at the time.

The taxi pulled up alongside the fish docks, then you carried all your gear on board.

The ship had that smell you can't describe. Every trawler had that smell. It was a smell that nearly made you sick. To me it was like the smell of death.

The next thing you'd notice would be the music coming from the party berth. It was usually country and western, often Patsy Cline!

Another reminder of what I'd run away from.

What I can recall was when you got on board there was a number of narrow alleyways leading to the different berths and sleeping quarters.

Down below there was an eight-man berth. Oh it really stunk! Booze - you could smell the rum, you could smell the whisky, even from outside.

You could see these men, brave men, hard as nails men, sailing on this rust bucket. Most men took beer away with them. But you'd find the officers of the ship never drank at the time the ship was leaving from Hull to sail to the fishing grounds off the coast of Norway.

That would be a three to four day steam. So it was rare if we saw the skipper, mate, second mate or the bosun drinking. Because it was their job to get us to the fishing grounds.

My job aboard the St Dominic was galley boy. That meant working in the kitchen, up at 5.30 every morning, no matter what the weather was like!

When they let go of those ropes and your ship left Hull for

those three weeks or more, there was no turning back. You couldn't go home. That was it. That was your life.

Oh, sea-sickness! Don't let me tell you about that! It would put you off your food.

It did me for about a week on my first trip to sea. It was like having a never-ending nightmare. One you couldn't wake up from! From the moment that ship set sail it would somehow make you want to be sick. And when the ship started to roll in them rough waters you could not help but be sick twenty-four hours a day for the first three days. There was no escape!

Believe me, when you get sea-sickness, all you want to do is curl up and die. But there's no hiding place aboard a sidewinder deep sea trawler.

Oh, I still had to peel spuds, clean all the pots and pans, do all the washing up, clean where all the crew ate, then clean their berths. You were on call all day!

My first trip, well the first six days at least, were the worst anyone could ever go through! Until the ship started fishing. Once the nets were in the water and the ship was nice and steady, you started to get your sea legs...

Well once my kitchen duties were done, about 8 o'clock on the night, I was allowed to go work down in the fishroom, where the fish would be stored on ice.

It gave me the chance to see what the life of a fisherman was like. Let me tell you there is a bond amongst trawlermen that I have never seen before or since.

I admit it wasn't always easy to appreciate. One minute they could be fighting with each other, the next they were the best of mates. But when it came to the crunch they'd all stick together. They'd do anything for one another. When fishing got into full swing, after about ten days, you'd see the true spirit of those men. They were hard men - and I mean hard men.

I remember on my first trip we had been fishing very well. Working eighteen hours non-stop with six hours sleep, for the full ten days. Eighteen hours work, six hours sleep, that's if you got the six hours sleep. It was hard work but I loved it.

It was like that for about ten days solid. We had a good trip and a good catch!

After the work came party time! The booze was in full flow.

The Lambs Navy Rum came out. I was allowed to join in the party. Most of the crew knew my Dad and my brother, David and my cousins - that helped me.

Well the first party I'd seen at sea got out of control. Words turned into fists. Fists turned into a glass - smashed into a man's face. Then I watched as the man started to remove the glass splinters out of his face and say to the guy that smashed the glass into his face, 'Is that the best you can do?'

Then he hit him with the perfect right! What a punch! Party over! When the guy came round he went straight back to work. Nowt said! Everything was just back to normal. What a life! Best of mates they were...

What a life!

They say you never forget your first trip to sea. I certainly didn't forget mine.

To top it all when we were twenty-four hours from home, one guy threw himself overboard. He was never seen again. It was all because he owed somebody some money back at home. They said the guy thought the 'warrant man' would be waiting for him, but he wasn't.

All that - and plenty more - happened on my very first trip to sea. I don't have to tell you that three weeks away really opened my eyes.

We spent over twenty-four hours searching for that guy who went missing over the side. All the ships and trawlers in the area searched for that brave man. But in those seas there was no chance of finding him and the poor soul was never seen again!

I picked up loads of money, mainly back-handers.

All the crew picked up good money. We had a good trip. Good fish, big money. Big, big money!

I think I got about £500. That was a huge amount of money for a teenager back in the early 1970s. Imagine what the other guys must have picked up! And bear in mind at the time my brother Trevor was earning £35 a week.

Mally with £500 in his hands. King for a day. King for the days I was at home. King for going through all that I'd been through. I deserved to go for a drink with the crew when I got home and picked my money up, I thought. That was our day. The day we picked our money up. That was our day. We'd earned it...

Life was like that on Hessle Road. Hessle Road was world famous. I'd say the hardest men in Hull were born and bred on Hessle Road. And they weren't all fishermen that came from Hessle Road. I know it was the heart of the fishing industry. I'll reflect on my fishing days and Hessle Road much more later in my story because it was a way of life.

The life of a deep-sea trawlerman became my way of life. You had to be hard to go to sea. In some ways it helped me to be what I am today. But in others it was the cause for me going down those wrong roads in life.

Remember what you see is what you get with me.

I never got much time to get the 'thinks' on while I was on my first trip to sea. Yes, I naturally did think about Karen. But when I did, all I could see was that good-looking wanker chatting-up my girlfriend...

As soon as I got home, I went round to Karen's. I think we went shopping. Karen was not allowed in the pubs but I was. So when Karen went home to her Mam and Dad's, I went out on the piss. I was only home for three days and then it was back to sea again! I took my brother, Trevor, out drinking. By then, he'd also left number 11. He was living with one of my older brothers, Raymond. But poor Bobby was still at home with 'big bad John'.

No matter what, whenever I was 'at home', I always went to see my Mother. My Father allowed that. But I'd always go when he was out. I didn't want to meet me Dad again until later on in life.

Me and Karen were looking for somewhere of our own to live. Our Trevor was also looking for somewhere so I said look for a house for us all to share and I'll pay the deposit...

I went back to sea on the St Dominic for another three trips of three weeks at a time. I got used to the sea-sickness. I got my sea legs. And once we got to the fishing grounds, I loved it.

I didn't like the parties on board the ship, they always led to fights, which I was soon to become a part of. Remember, no man was going to knock me out again.

Well it soon came to the point where I was put to the test. I had to live up to that statement!

Party time on board the St Dominic.

164

Everybody was happy. But then one wanker got up. A hardcase. And he said to me, 'Hey Mally, I sailed with your Dad. And everyone on board your Dad's ship were shit scared of your Dad, except one man - and that was me!'

I replied, Everyone aboard this ship seems shit scared of you, barring one man, I said.

'Who would that be?' he asked.

That would be me, I replied.

Well this guy was known as an hardcase. And it was said if he takes his glasses off, run!

Well I said I didn't fear him. He started to remove his glasses. But by the time he put his hand on his glasses, I'd hit him with a straight right! My fist right in his face. Followed with a left, then another right. Before he knew it I'd knocked him out.

A legend - I'd put him to sleep.

Don't fuck with me, I was screaming, while I continued to rain the blows on him. I gave him what my old man gave me!

I had to sleep with my eyes open that trip but we made friends shortly after and have remained friends ever since.

So at the age of seventeen, I'd already knocked out a 'hardcase' of the fishing industry. I was already labelled. That was it. Welcome to the world of deep-sea trawlers...

Who is this young Welburn?

Oh, don't mess with him - don't mess with the Welburns - they're fucking mad!

But it didn't stop there of course. Every time I came home from sea someone somewhere wanted to fight me. And with me getting them five meals a day and with all that hard work and all that exercise I was getting, I was built like that brick shithouse we've all heard about! I feared no man. I couldn't wait to challenge my Father. But he was still that mountain. So fighting my Father would come later in life...

Time passed very quickly. Karen had our baby boy. We named him Peter David.

One time, you know I remember I came home from sea and I saw the slime-ball holding my baby.

Karen told me we were through. I couldn't believe it. I didn't want to believe it.

I told her to get my baby off that slime-ball.

Well he challenged me, didn't he. One punch! Goodnight!

She didn't want to see me anymore. And she refused to let me see my child again too!

She was on her own for a while, about a couple of years, living with Peter at her Mam's house. And I think she then moved in at her Nanna's.

Her Nanna was another lovely lady.

The next thing I knew Karen was courting with someone else. But by that time of course I'd fallen in love with my next girlfriend, Kerry-Anne, who would become my wife. Later still Karen also got married and moved out of town - and then moved back again. And it wasn't until about six years further down the line that our paths crossed again.

It was through the CSA, the child maintenance people, because Karen had now got a job and they came after me for maintenance.

In those days they did a blood test. And the results proved that I was the father of young Peter. I think I was on a walkabout then - that's when you're laid off from a ship. Then I had to go to court for the maintenance ruling. The maintenance was £5 a week then, which was virtually the same as family allowance. So the difference was that when I was out of work and she was getting £4.95 family allowance, I was told to pay five pence a week!

That's how it worked, I paid £5 a week when I was in work and five pence a week when I wasn't...

Shortly after me and Karen split up I was offered the chance to sail on a ship that was going away for ten weeks. It was a freezer trawler. It caught the fish and froze it at sea which allowed it to stay at sea for up to two and a half months.

The skipper was Arthur Ball. The ship was the St Jason.

Away for two and a half months? I jumped at the chance of being a 'decky learner' - a 'snacker', working on the deck, learning how to mend the nets and stuff. I didn't like that part so much. I'm no good 'round the edges'. That's a fisherman's saying. But I loved throwing them twelve stone blocks of frozen fish about. It was another paid 'work-out'. And all what I could eat - and get paid £30 a week, over thirty years ago.

Our Trevor was on about £40 but I couldn't spend mine. Also, I was on a small percentage of the catch plus back-handers. It all added up. And ten weeks wages, 'behind the clock' as we used to say, was a lot of money.

Even if we caught no fish at all, I went home to my wages. That's where the saying, 'Three Day Millionaires' came from. King for a day, that one day. That one day when you'd been away for ten weeks and then you got home and picked up all your wages. And all your money from the sale of the fish. All your money from back-handers. Put it all together and hold it all in your hand in cash. Then go out and party! Who was going to stop me? Plenty tried and plenty fell by the wayside...

I'd get into fights every time I came home. It was the way of life. I lost count of the number of men who came to me for a fight. They'd say things like, 'Are you Mally Welburn and do you think you can fight? If so, I want to fight you.'

My reply was, listen, one of us is going to taste hospital food and one is going to taste prison food. Now fuck off!

But would they? No! So what do you do? What did I do? I told them again - but still no joy.

So I just banged them. Bang! Goodnight! All I did was picture my Father in front of me. It worked every time!

Just imagining me Dad and what he used to do to me. And most of all, what he used to do to my Mother!

Anyway one trip while I was away I got a telegram. I'd only been at sea for two weeks of the ten weeks trip.

Getting a telegram was a special occasion at the time because that was the modern technology. They cost a lot of money to send so it was usually something important. Your mother's dead or Merry Christmas for instance! Well when I got my telegram the skipper said, 'Your brother's been in touch.'

Our Trevor? I said.

'Yes,' he said, 'He wants to know if he can borrow a couple of hundred quid? He's got the chance of a house and he needs it for a deposit. Will you allow us to let him have it?'

The single guys had this saying that our wages were 'behind the clock'. The married blokes had to go home and get their 'settlings', which was the percentage of the catch. I used to come home with £3-400 when I'd been on those ten-week trips. So we sent a telegram back giving Trevor permission to go down and get the £200.

He said he'd found a nice house to let but needed the money for the deposit. He couldn't find that kind of money cos he'd been laid off work and was only getting sommat like £10 a week dole money. I was getting £30 a week left in the office for that one day - live for the day!

Our kid also said that Bobby had been kicked out of number 11 by me old man and had nowhere to live. I'd been expecting that cos once you got to sixteen, no matter what, as far as me Dad was concerned, you were out! You were on your own. There's the door my lad, off you go! And a nice little push - just a tender little push - to send you on your way.

Again what could I do?

I allowed Trevor to go and get £200 in advance of my wages. But we had a bad trip. Ten weeks away and we didn't catch enough fish to cover costs. The ship kept breaking down, which was good in a way because we got to visit Norway. But that was all.

When we got alongside the quay at Hull there was Trevor, my twin, 'Rigsby' - tight as a duck's arse!

My twin. My twin. Standing there, waiting for me. Why? I wondered. I soon found out! It was to tell me about the house we were renting. No sooner had I jumped off the ship to greet my twin, he said, 'I need to tell you I borrowed that £200 off you and I will give you it back.'

You what, I said.

'But the house is mine and I don't want you living there, my bird has moved in with me,' he said.

I said give me my money back now!

'I'll give you it back at £5 a week,' he replied.

Fuck that - I just banged him! But unbeknown to me the coppers were hiding around the corner. My brother had informed them that I was going to hit him. How right he was! I was locked up overnight! My first night home for ten weeks and my own brother got me locked up all over a house. All over him owing me £200! So he could have a nice place for him and his girlfriend. The wanker!

I was not allowed near his house, the one I'd given him the money for. I was banged up until the morning. Then I was up before the judge the same day! And guess who the judge was? You've got it! The one that sent me away to the children's home. The one who hated fishermen!

When I was called up before the court, Trevor was there.

The Judge asked me why I'd hit my brother? But he didn't listen to my side of the story, he took our Trevor's side. I asked the Judge what I should do about the £200 that Trevor owed me.

'That's nothing to do with me,' he said. 'You're up for assault on your brother. The money is a civil matter.'

He told me to go through the small claims court to get my money back off my twin. Where do I live then Judge? I asked. He told me I could go to prison while my ship was ready to sail. Or I could go sleep aboard my ship. Or I could make it up with my brother.

I replied, I'd sooner sleep on the street than make it up with a brother who had just had me over for £200!

'Well here's a £100 fine for you as well, now get out!' That was the Judge!

I swear I was going to knock our Trevor out. Then he said, 'You can stay while you go back to sea.'

'Rent free?' I asked.

'No, I can't let you stay rent free,' he replied.

Then take it off the money you owe me, I said. I'll pay you £10 a week, seven days, knock it off the £200 you owe me I said!

Well the deal was I was to get my own grub. I was not allowed any of their food whatsoever, absolutely nothing, I couldn't even use their milk, tea or bread!

The sly bastard would leave me notes telling me that there were twelve slices of bread, four eggs and twenty-four potatoes left. He even marked the side of the bottle of milk but I got around that by topping the milk up with a drop of water. What I also liked to do was to get a sewing needle and prick the ends of his eggs and blow the egg out. That would really fuck his brain up!

There were other little notes - dos and don'ts - all over the house, the house that he'd got with my money!

The house was down a terrace in Subway Street, off Hessle Road. The terrace had four houses on either side. Mine was the end one at the bottom of the terrace. Subway Street was just like any other street except there was no street-lighting. So on a night the whole terrace was always pitch dark. But it was my first house. My first real home. It had a big bay window at the front. And a lovely, little old couple lived next door.

My brother, Trevor, was shit scared of the dark. He had been since he was a small boy. And even down Subway Street, he used to sleep with the light on in his bedroom. He would have nine locks on his bedroom door. On the inside of each door there were maybe three types of locks.

Oh, he's a black belt, fifth dan, now in karate. But believe me, that house only had two rooms downstairs and two bedrooms upstairs, with a kitchen and an outside toilet but there were more locks in that little house than there are in your average prison!

I had to sleep in the room downstair, which was to the left as soon as you came through the front door. Then to the right was a door that led you into the main living room. There was a bay window in the living room with a three-seater settee across the bay. So we had to stand on the settee to close the curtains.

Opposite the settee was the telly. And oh, guess what? Our kid also had a little coffee table - the same as me old man's!

The kitchen was in a lean-to veranda. I'll give our kid his dues, the house was cosy and he kept it nice and tidy. But I was never allowed in his bedroom. He had four locks on the outside of his bedroom door and another five on the inside. So when he was out you couldn't get into his room and when he was in, you definitely couldn't get in.

Well one night our kid brought his bird down for the night. By she was beautiful but our kid was always an arsehole with her! Well my ship wasn't due to sail for another three weeks because of engine trouble. We all had to sign on the dole.

I hated being at home with no money, all I could do was just hang around the house. But I would also go out with my trawler mates. We'd go drinking and usually end up fighting. I just didn't care! Not until I met the girl who came down one day with our Trevor's girlfriend.

I fell in love with her as soon as I set eyes on her. Her name was Kerry-Anne. I found out that her Dad was a skipper and her Mother was a lovely lady. But our Trevor did his best not to let me meet her.

Well I started to tidy up. I even bought me own bread, milk and eggs! I would fill the cupboard for our kid and I would say, what's in the cupboard is to share! He didn't know the meaning of the word sharing, hence his nickname, Rigsby, tight as a duck's arse! He would use both sides of the toilet paper.

I needed to see more of Kerry-Anne. I was eighteen, she was sixteen and had just left school. She'd been the best looking girl at Kingston High School and I was madly in love with her. I still had my face full of spots but she saw through them!

Well Kerry-Anne would come down with our kid's girlfriend and we would spend nights in playing records. And afterwards, I'd walk Kerry-Anne home to her posh house on Pickering Road.

I was in love all over again.

Our kid used to have his girlfriend sleep over - them upstairs in his room - me in the spare room downstairs. I just slept on a mattress. That was my bed, in a room with me clothes all over the place. Well that was me - untidy Mally. And of course 'spotless' Trevor was always on my case.

Keep the house tidy! Do this! Do that!

Well one morning I heard our Trevor get up early. It was only about 6 o'clock. He had got a new job to go to but his girlfriend, Janice, didn't go to work until 8 o'clock. I heard our kid say, 'See you later love. Lock the door and don't let our Mally in my bedroom!'

Well as soon as our kid had locked the front door behind him I sprang from my pit.

I went to the kitchen, put two eggs on to boil, put the kettle on and poured some cornflakes in a bowl.

Next I did two slices of toast. I got it all together and arranged it neatly on a tray. And I thought I'll give our kid's girlfriend her breakfast in bed.

Then I'll be in her good books and she would tell Kerry how thoughtful I was making her breakfast in bed, what woman doesn't like that?

So, I crept to the top of the stairs.

Oh, I'd also had a shave, cleaned my teeth and squeezed that spot that had appeared overnight. What a bonny sight I must have looked. I still had a face like that spotty dick pudding. But anyway you can but try...

Tray in hand, and feeling more than a little nervous, I stood outside our kid's bedroom door.

A quiet knock. Hello, good morning, I said, is it OK to come in? I've fetched you some breakfast. No answer...

A louder knock - but still no answer.

I tried to open the door and to my surprise the door opened. And I'll never forget the sight that greeted me on the other side...

There was nobody there! The bastard had set me up! And in his pink fucking room with his Elvis posters on every wall, there was a note pinned to his headboard that said,

GOT YER! KEEP OUT MY BEDROOM!

Well I got a breakfast out of it. But we fell out big style after that! Trevor thought I was after his girlfriend. He would never leave her in the same room as me - and not just me - any man! A bit like me Dad. He told me to leave. And I left.

My ship wasn't ready for another week. But how was I going to get to meet Kerry-Anne again now? I wondered.

Simple! I just went to her house and told her Mother I loved her daughter.

It was a bit of a shock for her Mother, Pat. But I can say if there was any Mother In Law that I could have wished for it would have been Pat Milner, nee Rodgers. That lovely lady has guided me in the right direction on more than one occasion. I'd put Pat in the same league as Karen's mother, Audrey. And Pat was to play a major role in the next stage of my life because she did end up being my Mother in Law.

Our kid kicked me out but little did he know when I left he took the wrong front door key off me! Well there was that many! I had nowhere to go. I was skint. And there were still five days to go before I set sail on a ten-week voyage...

I was seeing Kerry-Anne most nights but I had nowhere to sleep. I remember I slept on the park bench on the first night. But the second day I thought, fuck it, I'm going back to our kid's. I was paying for that house - and I'd only got a few days left before I'd be going away.

Well I waited until I saw our kid leave to go to his girlfriend's. It was about 7 o'clock and I knew he wouldn't be back until about 11.

Well, in for a penny in for a pound, I thought.

Now remember how shit scared of the dark our kid is!

The key I had opened the front door.

Bingo - I was in. Turn to the right - the living room. He'd left all the lights on and the curtains drawn.

I raided his kitchen. There were six eggs in a box.

I cracked them all into a glass, with a drop of milk - down in one go, lovely!

Right I'd had my fill. Now then, get hidden.

Where would our kid look when he comes in?

He wouldn't look behind the settee, would he?

Well I got settled behind the settee and waited for his return. It was quite a tight squeeze behind there with little space to move. And the curtain was covering me as well, there was little chance he'd spot my hiding place. After an hour or so I heard a whistle outside and our kid's voice. He was shouting, 'Come on Rommy, come on boy!'

Had he got me Dad's dog with him? Had he been round to me old man's?

Where did he get a dog from? But I soon realised he never had the dog of course.

He pretended to have a dog with him on a night, when he was returning to that house, coming down that dark terrace.

After all that murder had only been a couple of streets away. Anyone could jump out on you in the dark. It used to shit our Trevor up, big time! He would jump out of his skin and run a mile if he heard a strange noise. Just the rustle of some leaves, and he would shit himself!

So just imagine him coming down that terrace, whistling for a dog he never had. What state must he have been in?

'Come on Rommy, good dog! Get in there Rommy - that's it - good dog!' he shouted.

And there was me, behind the settee. I remember at first thinking, will the dog sniff me out?

After all I had saved Rommy's life remember. I pulled him out of that park lake. I rescued him from that swan. And I got a good hiding for it, but never mind. Anyway it would have been great to see him again, the dog that is, instead of just listening to our Trevor pretending he was there.

The next thing I heard was our kid putting his key in the lock. I'm behind the settee, hoping he doesn't find me.

Well as the door opened, in bounced our kid doing his karate moves and high-pitched screams.

'WHYYAARRGH! WHYYAARRGH!' And in two moves
he'd crossed the living room and was at the kitchen door. He
opened the six bolts on the door and switched the light on all
in those two quick moves, screaming at the same time, 'Get in
there, Rommy - kill!'

That was our kid's entrance, I found out that night. He must
have gone through that performance every time he got home!
He was shit-scared of living on his own. Our kid was one of
those people that when he saw Dracula or Frankenstein or
Doctor Jeckyll and Mr Hide on telly, he'd grab a cushion and
put it to his eyes so he didn't have to see them. He was living
on his nerves. He certainly was that night!

Well, when he found out nobody was hiding in the house and
after he had checked behind every door, accompanied by more
karate kicks and screams, he jumped on the settee and
punched the curtains in case someone was hiding behind
them. How he never saw me and how I stopped myself
bursting out laughing, I'll never know.

He calmed down a bit after that and started to whistle to
himself. Happy tunes.

We now know he didn't have a dog. But I could smell fish and
chips. Why you can always smell fish and chips a mile off,
can't you? A bit like smelling that freshly cooked chicken -
mmmmm - yum yum! And I could tell he was buttering his
bread. You always got your fish and chips wrapped up in
newspaper, didn't you? And you always ate them out of the
paper, didn't you? They tasted ten times as good like that!

Well he came back into the living room with his supper on a
tray. Bread and butter and a pot of tea.

Fortunately he hadn't noticed the missing eggs which he kept
in the box on the kitchen cupboard.

Then he put the telly on. It was all done in karate moves. Next,
I could feel him falling onto the settee with his supper
balanced on his lap. And then I could hear him eating it. I
listened to what was on the telly, it was the 'midnight movie'.
It was a horror film, a vampire movie, something like Dracula.
Perfect, I thought. I could tell by the music when it was
getting to 'shit your pants time'. And I could tell by our kid's
movements he was already 'shitting' himself!

I could tell he had stopped eating. He was probably already

behind a cushion. The music got louder. I could feel the settee getting pushed further and further back - and my hiding place getting smaller and smaller.

I could now see the back of our kid's head above the back of the settee. And when it came to that moment in the film where you dared not look, I calmly reached up and stroked the back of his neck.

The whole room seemed to explode!

I'd never seen anyone jump so high.

Or heard anyone scream so loud.

And I'd never seen anyone look so terrified or spin round in mid air quite like Trevor did.

Or seen fish and chips stuck to the ceiling like his were...

I popped my head over the back of the settee and said,

Now then Trevor, how's it going?

He held his hands to his chest. I thought he was having a heart attack. You'd have thought he'd seen a ghost. He was trembling. He did shit himself that night!

I said, Well I've only come for my gear. I'll get going now.

But he begged, and I mean really begged me not to go.

Well how could I go - only two more days and I'd be back at sea.

I stayed for those two days at our Trevor's. And I had the run of the house. He didn't want me to go back to sea, he didn't want me to go anywhere ever again. But I didn't want a nine to five job. No, that wasn't for me.

Oh, I was in love with Kerry-Anne.

But it was time to go to sea again...

I'll finish there for the early years of my life.

I know I bounce about a bit.

But I hope you enjoyed the first part of my story.

There's another two to follow about the rest of my life.

The next part is all about my fighting, my boozing, my gambling, my time in prison, my marriage, my divorce, my daughters, my son, my rise through the ranks of the fishing industry, my brothers, my Mam - and facing up to my Dad!

See you - Mally.

PS Don't forget there's a donation made to the NSPCC for every copy of this book sold, so don't pass it on to your friends. Let them buy it like you did. The more we sell the more we make - depending on what the big boys take off me.

Thanks - Mally

**Please leave your
comment at
www.mallywelburn.co.uk**